SO BLACK AND BLUE

SO BLACK

■ ■

THE UNIVERSITY OF CHICAGO PRESS
CHICAGO AND LONDON

AND BLUE

**RALPH ELLISON
AND THE
OCCASION OF
CRITICISM**

. . . .

KENNETH W. WARREN

KENNETH W. WARREN is professor of English at the University of Chicago. He is the author of *Black and White Strangers: Race and American Literary Realism*, published by the University of Chicago Press.

The University of Chicago Press, Chicago 60637
The University of Chicago Press, Ltd., London
© 2003 by The University of Chicago
All rights reserved. Published 2003
Printed in the United States of America
12 11 10 09 08 07 06 05 04 03   1 2 3 4 5
ISBN: 0-226-87378-1 (cloth)
ISBN: 0-226-87380-3 (paper)

Library of Congress Cataloging-in-Publication Data

Warren, Kenneth W.
    So black and blue : Ralph Ellison and the occasion of criticism /
Kenneth W. Warren.
        p.   cm.
Includes index.
    ISBN 2-226-87378-1 (cloth : alk. paper)—ISBN 0-226-87380-3
(paper : alk. paper)
    1. Ellison, Ralph—Criticism and interpretation.   2. Politics and
literature—United States—History—20th century.   3. Literature and
society—United States—History—20th century.   4. African American
men in literature.   5. African Americans in literature.   I. Title.
PS3555.L625 Z945 2003
818'.5409—dc21   2003005230

.... *In Memoriam* ....

Leon Forrest
Joe Wood

CONTENTS ·······················

ACKNOWLEDGMENTS ··················

No matter how much time one spends alone tapping out words on a keyboard, authorship is never a solitary undertaking. In writing this book, I have benefited from leave time supported by the University of Chicago and the Franke Institute for the Humanities. In addition, audiences at the John F. Kennedy—Institut für Nordamerikastudien at the Freie Universität Berlin, the University of Chicago's workshop on Race and the Reproduction of Racial Ideologies, the English departments at the University of Virginia and the City University of New York, where I presented various portions of this work, provided me with valuable feedback. I'd also be remiss here if I didn't mention Jeff Rice, who for several years pestered me to write on Ralph Ellison. And as this book wended its way toward completion at the University of Chicago Press, the responses from my readers and the copyediting of Erin DeWitt made the final product much better than it would have otherwise been.

Crucially important to shaping the trajectory of this book have been my ongoing conversations about African American literature and intellectual history with Adolph Reed Jr., Madhu Dubey, Rolland Murray, and Xiomara Santamarina. Adolph, in particular, as a friend and intellectual colleague, has been an ongoing source of insight, common sense, and, when necessary, consolation. His intellectual contribution to this project has been enormous.

Above all, however, the support and inspiration of my wife, Maria, and my children, Lenora, Mercedes, Marcus, and Gregory have been essential. Without them there would be little point in doing any of this.

Finally, the late Joe Wood was also one of the friends who suggested that I write a book about Ralph Ellison—a suggestion prompted by a somewhat incoherent draft of an article that I sent him during the time he worked as an editor at the *Village Voice*. Joe wisely put the article aside and sent me back to the drawing board. Unfortunately I didn't get right to work, and Joe passed on before I could inflict any of these pages on him. I don't know, therefore, if what I have produced here is what he had in mind, but under the circumstances, this must stand as the best I could do.

INTRODUCTION . . . .

Two days after the U.S. Supreme Court repudiated the nation's doctrine of "separate but equal" with its unanimous *Brown* v. *Board of Education* ruling, Ralph Ellison wrote a letter to Morteza Sprague expressing unexpected ambivalence at the news. Hard at work on his second novel, Ellison admitted to Sprague—who as chair of the English department at Tuskegee Institute had figured prominently in Ellison's intellectual development—that a touch of apprehension had leavened his elation. He lamented the way the Court's unanimous ruling had gotten "all mixed up with this book I'm trying to write, and it left me twisted with joy and a sense of inadequacy." He continued:

> Why did I have to be a writer during a time when events sneer openly at your efforts, defying consciousness and form? Well, so now the judges have found and Negroes must be individuals and that is hopeful and good. What a wonderful world of possibilities are unfolded for the children! For me there is still the problem of making meaning out of the past and I guess I'm lucky I described Bledsoe before he was checked out. Now I'm writing about the evasion of identity which is another characteristically American problem which must be about to change. I hope so, it's giving me enough trouble.[1]

Ellison clearly welcomed the *Brown* decision as a sea change in black-white race relations in the United States. No longer would the question of the Negro's humanity hang in the balance while social scientists and politicians deliberated. With the nation apparently ready to face the race problem squarely, young black Americans seemed poised to step into a world very different from the one that had fashioned the destinies of their parents.

Yet this step forward had precipitated, or at least exacerbated, what was to become for Ellison a decades-long artistic crisis. In creating Dr. Bledsoe, the high-handed college president who sends the protagonist of *Invisible Man* running from disaster to disaster, Ellison felt that as a novelist he had managed, in the nick of time, to strike off an indelible image of the Negro college president–*cum*–race leader before that figure had been "checked out" from history's vanguard. Not simply a creature of Ellison's imagination, Bledsoe embodies Jim Crow political reality as a man who was "more than just a college president. He was a leader, a 'statesman' who carried our problems to those above us, even unto the White House; and in days past he had conducted the President himself about the campus."[2] The Court's ruling presumably had changed this reality, making it highly unlikely that any future so-called race leader would emerge from the administrative ranks of the southern Negro college as had Booker T. Washington—to whom Bledsoe is an heir.

If in Bledsoe, Ellison had captured a bit of American reality, he had done so, it seemed, only as that reality was passing into history. Now as he struggled with the second novel, which he presciently focused on the voice of a black southern preacher, Ellison worried that there might not be even the nick of time for his next vision to attain any adequacy to the present moment. If the responsibility of the twentieth-century American novelist was to represent society in ways that prodded and shamed the nation out of its moral evasions, then a society on the verge of a civil rights revolution might have gotten out in front of its novelistic chroniclers.

In a larger sense, Ellison's remarks to Sprague betray an anxiety familiar to any writer of great ambition wrestling with the problem of how to write a "contemporary" novel that could remain meaningful long after the events it chronicles have lost their urgency—that is, how to prevent an old novel from becoming old news. To be effective as social critique, such a novel has to engage substantively the issues of its day; to resonate as literature, such a novel has to reach beyond the immediacy of its moment. *Invisible Man*'s reputation would suggest that Ellison is one of those few to have succeeded in this struggle. The 1953 National

Book Award was only the first of many honors bestowed on *Invisible Man*. Over a decade after the novel's publication, a critics' poll declared the book to be the most distinguished American novel published in the last fifty years. And in the 1980 issue of the *Carleton Miscellany* devoted to Ellison's work, Nathan A. Scott voiced the sentiments of his fellow critics and scholars by observing, "No other text of these past years has so lodged itself in the national imagination as has Mr. Ellison's great book: it stands today as the preeminent American novel of our period."[3] Yet despite the novel's immediate success, we find Ellison, scarcely two years after *Invisible Man*'s publication, wondering if one of his most memorable characters had been "checked out" by social change. Even if Ellison had been premature in predicting that *Brown* had ushered in a revolution in the nation's racial mores and politics, what did his worry say about *Invisible Man* in general? Had his novel succeeded in being merely topical rather than timeless?

In the introduction to *Shadow and Act*, his first collection of essays, Ellison describes his essays as "occasional pieces, written for magazines . . . to reduce my thinking—indeed, often to discover what I *did* think—to publishable form."[4] No surprise here. The essay as a form is occasional, exploratory, and provisional. Novels, however, are grander enterprises. What might it mean, then, to think of Ellison's only completed novel as likewise an "occasional piece"? What might it mean to regard Ellison not as a writer for the ages but rather as simply an extraordinary writer for the particular era in which he lived a good portion of his life—the roughly six decades of a legally Jim Crow American society?

This ought to be saying quite a bit in a nation still reckoning with the consequences of having committed itself for most of its history to social and economic practices and policies that depended on and ratified racial inequality. Any writer who has helped—and can continue to help—clarify those consequences has done no small service. Even so, assigning Ellison and his novel to the ranks of the "occasional" seems unavoidably to diminish both. Ellison's grand art becomes, in this view, little more than artful propaganda; his effort to speak to and for the larger human condition remains overshadowed by a particular time-bound social problem. What makes this charge even more problematic is that for much of its history, African American literature as a whole has been criticized precisely for this "failing." Critics have often disparaged black writers for being too eager to sacrifice artistry for protest. As early as 1892, Anna Julia Cooper complained that didactic literature had for too long predominated in writing about the Negro and called instead for a more literary black fiction.[5] By the 1920s Alain Locke's introductory essay to his edited volume *The New Negro* disparaged the literature of most of his predecessors for being governed by concerns other than artistry. Then, in the 1950s, Ellison and James Baldwin famously chastised Richard Wright on this same point.[6] Wright and those who had followed him in the tradition of protest fiction had not taken concerns of craft seriously enough. The novels produced by these writers were compelling "now," but only because the issues they addressed remained intensely on the minds of their readers.

While critiques of this sort have most frequently been aimed at writers from politically subordinated groups, all novel writers were potential victims of the topical. Ellison described the novel as an artistic form that necessarily emerged from the contingencies of the moment to teeter hopefully on the cusp of timelessness. "The novel's medium consists in a familiar experience occurring among a particular people, within a particular society or nation," he wrote in one of his many reflections on his craft.[7] To connect successfully with its reader, a work of fiction must tap into "a body of shared assumptions concerning reality and necessity, possibility and freedom, personality and value, along with a body of feelings, both rational and irrational, which arise from the particular circumstances of their mutual society."[8] The novel's dependence on particular circumstances rendered it vulnerable to being muted or muffled by historical changes and political shifts. And yet, according to Ellison, novelists could not sidestep this peril by focusing solely on universal or timeless themes because novels achieved "universality, if at all . . . by amplifying and giving resonance to a specific complex of experience until, through the eloquence of its statement, that specific part of life speaks metaphorically for the whole."[9] If a novel were to reach the universal, it could do so only by making the transit through the specific and the particular. For this reason, *Invisible Man*'s eloquent evocation of the particularities of race in mid-twentieth-century America carried with it no guarantee that its patterns of experience would forever retain their significance and resonance. As the pace of social change accelerated, the likelihood that Ellison's novel—or, for that matter, any other novel—would achieve universal significance lessened as well. According to Morris Dickstein, the novelists of Ellison's era persisted in their commitment to the form "even as its boundaries blurred and its hold on readers diminished."[10] So while Ellison might have been right in claiming that all novels thrive "on change and social turbulence," those same conditions threaten to reduce individual novels, even the great ones, to little more than creatures of their respective moments.[11]

When political and social forces delve a gulf between one historical moment and the next so that what was once experienced immediately becomes available only as antiquarianism, the changes often strike us as losses and leave us feeling as if the secrets and passions that animated a prior era have forever escaped our grasp. The Proustian trauma of being unable to inhabit feelings we once cherished touches us all at one time or another. Yet what should we think if our estrangement from the past is the product of progressive political transformations? We are all familiar with Walter Benjamin's dictum "There is no document of civilization which is not at the same time a document of barbarism."[12] Perhaps less clear is how these words apply to those documents of civilization written precisely to expose and denounce history's barbarisms. These are works whose critical effectiveness requires that they share to some degree the norms they are challenging, so that in exposing a society's ills, they inevitably expose themselves as well. If a more just and egalitarian society is to be purchased with tone deafness not only to the artistic chords that once charmed us but also to those that moved us to action, who is to declare the tab not worth paying?

Certainly from the nineteenth century forward, commentators on democracy and aesthetics in the United States have predicted that democratic gains might have aesthetic costs. In considering the American stage, for example, Alexis de Tocqueville declared, "The drama of one period can never be suited to the following age if in the interval an important revolution has affected the manners and laws of the nation." Tocqueville singled out the drama as more immediately responsive to social change because "no portion of literature is connected by closer or more numerous ties with the present condition of society than the drama."[13] In theory, however, his claim could be applied to all aesthetic forms and even to literary language itself.[14] For example, Henry James in *The American Scene* (1907) predicted that while immigration might transform the American language into "the most beautiful on the globe and the very music of humanity," that music would hardly be one to which we are accustomed. He opined, "Whatever we shall know it for, certainly, we shall not know it for English—in any sense for which there is an existing literary measure."[15]

Frantz Fanon, speaking more directly to the way that political change was transforming African American culture, commented that as

> soon as the Negro comes to an understanding of himself, and understands the rest of the world differently, when he gives birth to hope and forces back the racist universe, it is clear that his trumpet sounds more clearly and his voice less hoarsely. The new fashions in jazz are not simply born of economic competition. We must without any doubt see in them one of the consequences of the defeat, slow but sure, of the southern world of the United States. And it is not utopian to suppose that in fifty years' time the type of jazz howl hiccuped by a poor misfortunate Negro will be upheld only by the whites who believe in it as an expression of negritude, and who are faithful to this arrested image of a type of relationship.[16]

Whatever the problems with Fanon's assessment of early jazz, his argument that the appreciation of certain jazz styles is necessarily tied to Jim Crow sensibilities is at once instructive and troubling. How firmly linked is the socioeconomic and political world we are trying to defeat to the musical and literary products shaped by it?

What makes such a question seem impertinent is a long-standing predisposition to stress those aspects of black culture in the United States that appear to have persisted across time and space. This persistence of styles, habits, and attitudes is then adduced as evidence of black cultural and social autonomy even within the straitened circumstances of slavery and segregation. No matter how one assesses such a claim, it is true that the image of the American Negro as a blank slate emerging from the horrors of the middle passage and plantation slavery is no longer sustainable. The New World societies created by the slave trade and plantation economies were amalgams of European, African, and Native American practices. Yet whatever importance is attached to African life prior to the arrival of Africans in the Americas, neither the

Negro nor the African as a distinct cultural and political entity has existed for time immemorial. Notwithstanding the vitality of the cultural practices that developed under slavery, the coming of emancipation, imperfect as it was, contributed further to re-creating the cultures of the varied populations of African descendants. The perpetually shifting nomenclature used to refer to African-descended populations in the United States—Negro, colored, black, African American, people of color, et cetera—points to something other than the "changing same" of a black experience across time.[17] If today we rarely write sentences containing such phrases as "On his side of the joke the Negro looks at the white man," this is not because we have become more sophisticated about matters of identity.[18] Rather, we may no longer speak in these terms because the social entity that once justified this terminology no longer exists. The epigraph/epitaph attached to Ellison's posthumous novel makes this point eloquently. *Juneteenth* is dedicated "To That Vanished Tribe into Which I Was Born: The American Negroes."[19] This poignant dedication suggests that the world that gave us Ralph Ellison may be coming to a close—albeit too slowly. Even so, now may be the time, before its felt reality disappears altogether, to write a history that does not revisit the sustaining beliefs and feelings of that "once-upon-a-time when we were Negro" simply to revitalize them or pay them homage.[20] Instead, the goal must be to understand these feelings in order to loosen their grip on the levers that control the present and the future. That is, while this study begins with Ellison's fear that the vital signs of *Invisible Man*'s world were growing ever fainter since the *Brown* decision, the overriding concern of these essays is that we've perhaps kept the patient too long on life support. To clarify, the point is not to criticize Ellison for having failed to be something other than he was, nor is it to suggest that we should make an effort to stop liking *Invisible Man*. Rather, the goal is to understand the *problématique* that gave rise to the artistic, political, philosophical, and intellectual concerns that made possible the phenomenon of *Invisible Man* as well as our liking of *Invisible Man*.

Taking seriously Ellison's (and presumably our own) desire to see American society move toward realizing its democratic ideals is to enter a thicket of contradictions. The desire to change a society is provoked partly by aesthetic or social experiences that allow us to glimpse a world more fulfilling and richer than the one we currently inhabit. The aesthetic objects, social movements, and identities that make such glimpses possible are not simply vehicles to the future; they are themselves objects of value and desire in the present. Their proven capacity to sustain us in the past may also kindle our desire to carry them with us into the future. But here a question raised by David Harvey comes into play: "Can the political and social identities forged under an oppressive industrial order of a certain sort operating in a certain place survive the collapse or radical transformation of that order?" Harvey's response is "No," because the "perpetuation of those political identities and loyalties requires perpetuation of the oppressive conditions that gave rise to them. Working-class movements may then seek to perpetuate or return to the conditions of oppression that spawned them."[21] To be sure, Harvey would have been more accurate if he had said *inadvertently* "perpetuate or return to the conditions of oppression that spawned them." His conclusion, nonetheless, is sobering.

The breakthroughs achieved by political movements and aesthetic innovations can also foster the belief that further advances require simple iteration. The history of the Civil Rights era can condition us to scan the horizon for the next Martin Luther King Jr. or Malcolm X, and to believe that we see them reincarnated wherever we happen to look on the contemporary social scene. Robin D. G. Kelley, for example, has predicted, "We might discover a lot more Malcolm X's—indeed, more El Hajj Malik El Shabazz's—hiding beneath hoods and baggy pants," and Michael Eric Dyson has picked up the theme in observing, "Although it may seem blasphemous to say so, there is a great deal of similarity between Martin Luther King, Jr., and a figure like Tupac Shakur."[22] These attempts by Kelley and Dyson to vindicate contemporary black youth through favorable comparisons with Civil Rights–era heroes may be laudable enough given the often negative portrayal of young black men throughout various popular media, but these arguments merely reproduce the dubious proposition that the remedy for racial inequality rests largely on the creation of new black leaders. Dyson writes, "If we acknowledge that King was an extraordinary man despite his faults, perhaps we might acknowledge that some of our youth have the same potential for goodness that King possessed."[23] True enough, perhaps, but his observation—hagiographic rather than historical, exemplary rather than analytical—assumes that the problems currently facing us are merely updated versions of the problems that faced someone like King.[24] Likewise, the history of modern African American literature can make us believe that we discern the next Ralph Ellison in any literary critic or novelist who insists Marxism, black nationalism, or liberalism are not complex enough to convey the realities of the black experience. We are enjoined to wait for a novel that, *mutatis mutandis*, does for our moment the very things that *Invisible Man* did for its own, ignoring the possibility that perhaps Ellison's novel was, as Kenneth Burke called it, "epoch-making" and as such would have no sequel, or that, to quote Dickstein again, after the 1950s "the novel itself was becoming less important."[25]

The story of Ellison is very much the story of modern American literature. There is no gainsaying the sense of breakthrough created by the literary movements of the 1920s and 1930s. American modernists gave us new ways of seeing and thinking about the world and about literature. But for all its innovation, this literature, too, was unavoidably a part of its historical moment, and connected to that moment in ways that may be disturbing to those of us who wish to find in this literature the values we wish to uphold. Walter Benn Michaels, for example, has argued that "the great American modernist texts of the '20s must be understood as deeply committed to the nativist project of racializing the American."[26] That is, notwithstanding the considerable aesthetic power of the work of William Faulkner, Ernest Hemingway, Willa Cather, F. Scott Fitzgerald, Nella Larsen, Alain Locke, and others, their writings cannot be disentangled from the dubious political work of justifying our commitment to different racial and ethnic identities. It is no accident, then, that assimilationist Jews like Robert Cohn are ostracized in *The Sun Also Rises* and that Tom Buchanan in *The Great Gatsby* voices eugenicist fears about the rise of darker races. In Michaels's view, modern literature has been deeply implicated in reproducing a society in which racial difference matters intensely. This literature has helped secure the paradoxical notion that what makes humans alike is that we all exist within groups each having its "own" equally valuable culture. Thus, while my culture as a black American is presumed to be neither better nor worse than the culture of someone who is Jewish, it is nonetheless understandable that I would prefer my culture because it is mine, just as a Jewish individual ought to prefer her culture because it is hers. Such, Michaels argues, is the key claim of the cultural pluralism that subtended American modernism, which though often understood as a way to avoid grounding human difference in race, does quite the opposite: "By understanding identity as the privileged object of social contest, pluralism makes race and culture structurally equivalent and formally interchangeable."[27] What Michaels argues, then, is that a good many of the 1920s American writers whose work emphasized cultural rather than biological differences between and among social groups unwittingly reinstalled racial difference as the best way to understand who we are as Americans.

Ellison's relationship to the writers mentioned by Michaels was inconsistent, often changing to fit the political or aesthetic occasion. At times, Ellison chided Steinbeck, Hemingway, and Faulkner for their moral evasiveness when it came to confronting the Negro, complaining that in their work the "conception of the Negro as a symbol of Man" that had been "organic to nineteenth-century literature" had been supplanted in twentieth-century American fiction by its opposite—the Negro as inhuman.[28] And though Ellison in other essays attempted to moderate this view (at one point he credited Hemingway with a sensibility that approached the blues),[29] he did return to this critique on occasion in order to say that however good the fiction produced by the Lost Generation might have been, "it was not good enough or broad enough to speak for today."[30]

Yet as illustrated by his relationship with Faulkner, Ellison's commitment to the centrality of the Negro as a symbol of humanity may have left him confined within some of the constraints that had hobbled the writers of the Lost Generation. Ellison knew better than his predecessors that southern conservatives had frequently forestalled political and legislative attempts to improve the status of black Americans by asserting that the social system of the south was rooted in a cultural differences highly resistant to change. As a student of the post-Reconstruction betrayal of black freedmen, he was well aware that the Supreme Court's "separate but equal" decision in 1896 rested on Justice Brown's contention that the quest for equality was beyond legislative and political remedy. Brown criticized the arguments put forth by Homer A. Plessy's legal team for assuming "that social prejudices may be overcome by legislation." On the contrary, Brown insisted, "We cannot accept this proposition. If the two races are to meet upon terms of social equality, it must be the result of natural affinities, a mutual appreciation of each other's merits and a voluntary consent of individuals."[31] Likewise the writings of William Graham Sumner, which exerted a powerful influence over sociology in the late nineteenth and early twentieth centuries, insist that "legislation can not make mores."[32] These views proved particularly useful in consolidating a white supremacist order in the south that justified itself by dramatizing the supposed disaster that accompanied black political action during the Reconstruction era.

Ellison never lost sight of the fact that the overthrow of Reconstruction was a supremely political act, accompanied by "mass violence against Negroes who were functioning in the legislatures."[33] Yet in his effort to hold literature morally responsible for the nation's ills, Ellison sometimes inadvertently dimmed his political insights. In faulting twentieth-century American literature for failing to represent the full depth of black experience in American history, Ellison often applauded Faulkner's work for its "continuity of moral purpose which made for the greatness of our classics." Singling out "The Bear" from *Go Down, Moses* for having brought us "as close to the moral implication of the Negro as Twain or Melville," Ellison calls our attention to the novella's fourth section, where "we find an argument in progress in which one voice (that of a Southern abolitionist) seeks to define Negro humanity against the other's enumeration of those stereotypes which many Southerners believe to be the Negro's basic traits."[34] This portion of the story, Ellison declares, is where "Faulkner makes his most extended effort to define the specific form of the American Negro's humanity and to get at the human values which were lost by both North and South during the Civil War."[35] Faulkner's "extended effort" takes the form of a lengthy conversation between the story's hero, Isaac (Ike) McCaslin, and his older cousin McCaslin Edmonds in which Ike justifies his decision not to inherit the land owned by his forefathers but to accept the moral burden of the past.

The unacknowledged irony in Ellison's admiration of section 4 of "The Bear" is that Ike's recognition of black humanity depends on some of the very same assumptions about history and the human condition that had in the first place contributed to obscuring the humanity of black people in the south. That is, Ike's moral heroism confirms a reading of the Reconstruction years as a tragic era when human action—more specifically, political action—necessarily proved unable to confer equality on the former slaves. Describing the period as a conflict among three "peoples"—white southerners, Negro ex-slaves, and white carpet-baggers, Faulkner's narrator paints Reconstruction as that

> dark corrupt and bloody time while three separate peoples had tried to adjust not only to one another but to the new land which they had created and inherited too and must live in for the reason that those who had lost it were no less free to quit it than those who had gained it were.

The narrative then first specifies the ex-slaves as "those upon whom freedom and equality had been dumped overnight and without warning or preparation or any training in how to employ it or even just endure it and who misused it not as children would nor yet because they had been so long in bondage and then so suddenly freed, but misused it as human beings always misuse freedom." This observation leads Ike to conclude, *"Apparently there is a wisdom beyond even that learned through suffering necessary for a man to distinguish between liberty and license."*[36]

Faulkner's Ike does not succumb to the racism of, say, a U. B. Phillips, who believed that "an African nature" persisted through plantation slavery and emancipation, thus reconciling the Negro to the social order of the south.[37] Nor does he blame the failure of Reconstruction on alleged black inadequacies created by the horrors of slavery. Rather, in Ike's view, the shortcomings that undermined Reconstruction were the result of inevitable human frailties: the former slaves "misused [freedom] as human beings always misuse freedom." The Negro was not a lesser human being but a being who embodied the essence of the human condition.

Such a view is clearly an enormous step forward from the standard histories of the Reconstruction era that charged the post–Civil War ills of the south to Negro corruption and venality. Yet by making the experience of the Negro neither more nor less than the condition of being human, and by making the sine qua non of humanity the misuse of freedom, "The Bear" inoculates history from political explanation and, to some degree, from history itself. Placing the capacity to "distinguish between liberty and license" beyond the experience of those upon whom fell the task of fashioning a free and equal society, Faulkner makes the failure of Reconstruction an inevitable human failure rather than an avoidable political one. Moral courage in "The Bear" presupposes the inadequacy of political action.

Ellison was ever ready, despite his admiration of Faulkner, to point out the shortcomings of the south's most important author. When the integration crisis of the 1950s caused Faulkner to write an open "Letter to the North" in *Life* magazine pleading that the south needed more time to adjust to Civil Rights gains, Ellison commented acerbically in a letter to Albert Murray that Faulkner

> forgets that Mose [Ellison's colloquial term for the Negro] isn't in the market for his advice, because he's been knowing how to "wait a while"—for over three hundred years, only he's never been simply waiting, he's been probing for a soft spot, looking for a hole, and now he's got the hole. Faulkner has delusions of grandeur because he really believes that he invented these characteristics which he ascribes to Negroes in his fiction.[38]

Crucial to Ellison's criticisms of Faulkner is the awareness that artistic insights have a way of turning into political liabilities. Faulkner's letter demonstrates that the moral authority derived from the novel is not always a reliable resource for informing political judgments. Yet what was clearly an affliction in Faulkner's case was not so readily apparent to Ellison when it came to his own readiness to reason from his fiction to real life.

Keeping in mind the vagaries of Ellison's relationship to his literary ancestors, I want to explore in these chapters the ways in which his work, like theirs, often abetted, even as it challenged the idea of a social order defined by racial difference. To echo Ellison's critique of the Lost Generation: however good his work may have been, it may not always be good enough or broad enough on its different frequencies to speak for U.S. society today. That is to say, the degree to which Ellison and these other writers remain capable of speaking for us may point less to their universality than to a broader social and political failure that keeps us mired in the racial commonsense of the twentieth century.

When Ellison died in 1994, he appeared to be enjoying a renascence as a cultural and political guide. In 1990 author Charles Johnson, in accepting the National Book Award for his novel *Middle Passage*, named Ellison as an influential ancestor. And along with Johnson, a covey of writers generally associated with Ellison's sensibilities—

Albert Murray, Stanley Crouch, and Leon Forrest—was garnering favorable, if sometimes controversial, attention for having resisted the balkanization that multiculturalism had supposedly inflicted on American life. Forrest—whose first novel, *There Is a Tree More Ancient than Eden*, had been hailed by Ellison—had just published his career-defining novel *Divine Days*. On the scholarly and critical front, Ellisonian sensibilities were evident. Shelley Fisher Fishkin, in her 1993 book *Was Huck Black?*, attracted national attention by producing evidence that Mark Twain had modeled Huck Finn's white southern vernacular on the speech of a young black boy who had been the subject of Twain's brief sketch "Sociable Jimmy." By way of accounting for her discovery, Fishkin credited none other than Ralph Ellison for "preparing and shaping my awareness of the role of African-American voices in Twain's art." According to Fishkin, Ellison knew that understanding "African-American traditions is essential if one wants to understand *mainstream* American literary history. And understanding mainstream literary history is important if one wants to understand African-American writing in the twentieth century."[39] Following Ellison's death, Stanley Crouch eulogized him in the *New Republic* as a gunslinger who "had always traveled on a ridge above the most petty definitions of race and had given us a much richer image of ourselves as Americans, no matter how we arrived here, what we looked like, or how we were made."[40]

Discernible in Crouch's lines is not merely an aesthetic doctrine but the lineaments of a politics that defined itself against the rise of Black Power during the late 1960s and early 1970s. Crouch's voice joined with a host of others lamenting "the fragmentation, resegregation, and tribalization of American life," to use the words of Arthur M. Schlesinger Jr., who brandished Ellison's writing at Afrocentrists in order to challenge the belief that black self-esteem required black role models.[41] Schlesinger reminded his readers that Ellison had derived his inspiration from such writers as Hemingway, Dostoyevsky, and Faulkner without compromising his racial identity. Noting that Ellison had discovered these writers in the library of Jim Crow–era Tuskegee Institute, Schlesinger worried that black students in the post-segregation-era New York public school system might find their curriculum more segregated than had their Jim Crow predecessors. By turning to Ellison, the nation just might stem this tide.

Agreeing largely with Schlesinger's line of thinking, Sean Wilentz hailed the advent of a "transracial understanding of American culture and politics" that had been "influenced by the writings of Ralph Ellison and Albert Murray." In Wilentz's view, transracialism creates "a broad identification with humanity over narrow racial solidarities. By challenging the political and cultural sanctity of 'blackness' (and, it must be added, of 'whiteness,' too), and by regarding America as a mulattoized culture of multicultural individuals, transracialists contradict the melodramatic racialist mystique that began to govern the American left during the Black Power enthusiasms of 30 years ago."[42]

Another curious contribution to this side of the debate is Norman Podhoretz's provocatively titled 1999 *Commentary* article, "What Happened to Ralph Ellison." In this essay Podhoretz declares himself no longer a big fan of *Invisible Man*, which he views as "dated," but a somewhat grudging admirer of Ellison nonetheless. Ellison's novel, Podhoretz avers, has many problems. Its central metaphor is "archaic" because "if Negroes—or blacks or African Americans—were once invisible, today, in the age of affirmative action and multiculturalism, they have become perhaps the most salient group in the American consciousness." Podhoretz also complains of an absence in the novel of so-called "black violence and criminality"—an absence that in his mind aligns the novel with the political trends that had made it difficult for even "the most sympathetic white liberals" to support black political and social agendas.[43] All was not lost, however, because in Ellison's essays, as "stilted and awkward and pretentious" as Podhoretz finds them, he also discerns "a tradition that exposes the aggressive black nationalists and separatists and mau-mauers who have grown more numerous today than ever for the whiners and braggarts and self-haters Ellison despised them as being."[44] Here, despite Ellison's alleged aesthetic lapses, was a writer whom even a neo-conservative like Podhoretz could love.

Perhaps the most banal celebration of the anti-nationalist Ellison came earlier in 1999 when Shelby Steele took advantage of the publication of *Flying Home and Other Stories by Ralph Ellison* to reprise portions of the argument he had put forward in *The Content of Our Character: A New Vision of Race in America* (1991) and *A Dream Deferred: The Second Betrayal of Black Freedom in America* (1999), both of which charge that African Americans as a group had become enamored of their status as victims and had adopted a strategy preoccupied with evoking white guilt. In his review of Ellison's short fiction, Steele predictably views Ellison's work as an antidote to this political illness that surfaced most visibly in protest literature, which because it "was written above all else to trigger white obligation, . . . could not examine the strengths of black culture without putting that obligation at risk. A chief characteristic of black protest writing, therefore, is the concealment of black culture and black ingenuity so as not to diffuse obligation." Steele claims that he had been forced to read *Invisible Man* "a little on the sly" because the "literary Ellison did not even warrant consideration" from his peers who were enamored of works like Eldridge Cleaver's *Soul on Ice*.[45]

Portrayed as a ray of light against a backdrop of "black group 'truth,'" "melodramatic racial mystique," and "aggressive black nationalists," Ellison emerges for writers like Wilentz, Steele, and Podhoretz as a transracial messiah heralding the return of humanism and reason to redeem an American society threatened by racial medievalism.

A major problem with this account, though, is that Ellison had never really disappeared from the scene in such a way as to support the claim of his second coming. While as a novelist he may have been buried beneath the massive manuscript of his second, uncompleted novel, Ellison, as a cultural authority, had remained in view from the 1950s until his death. Nor was Ellison's public persona always the unambiguous transracial champion that these writers discern. Neither the novel nor the essays consistently contradict the Black Power "mystique" that troubles Wilentz. In fact, if 1990s "transracialists" have traced their lineage from Ellison, so, too, have some Black or neo–Black Aestheticians, who define themselves not through a broad identification with Western humanism but through their conviction that the full development of black American literature and culture requires the elaboration of norms and ideals from within the experience of black Americans. On this point, Leon Forrest astutely reminded the *New Yorker* in 1994 that whatever claims transracialism might make about him, Ellison had always been a "race man." Forrest explains: "A race man means you're in a barbershop conversation, and there might be a nationalist, an N.A.A.C.P. man, whatever, but they're all concerned with getting African-Americans ahead in the community. I know Ralph had a lot of respect for many of the things Adam Clayton Powell stood for at first. . . . Ralph is for a robust onslaught against racism but, at the same time, for building within the race."[46] And well before Forrest, Harold Cruse in his monumental corrective critique of black nationalism took various nationalists to task for their failure to see that "even if Ellison did express the view that literature and art are not racial . . . the evidence remains that all of Ellison's work as exemplified in *Invisible Man* and *Shadow and Act* is definitely racial."[47]

In fact, many of the critics associated with the Black Aesthetic line of thinking kept *Invisible Man* on their critical radar during the late 1960s and early 1970s. Addison Gayle's 1969 edited volume *Black Expression*, George E. Kent's *Blackness and the Adventure of Western Culture* (1972), and Arthur P. Davis's *From the Dark Tower* (1974) all include commentary on Ellison's artistry, and many of these authors worked hand in glove with writers whom Steele would describe as being blinded by "race-focused group truth." Kent's book, which was published by Haki Madhubuti's Third World Press, includes a lengthy discussion of the Jim Trueblood section of *Invisible Man* and, contrary to Steele's contention, celebrates black folk culture.

To be sure, Ellison often encountered great personal hostility from black students during his visits to college campuses in the 1960s and 1970s. And yet, there has persisted, even in this vilification, a strain of recognition that Ellison could not be so easily dismissed as a racial sell-out. Larry Neal—who was central in the 1960s and early 1970s to the Black Arts movement—concludes that there "is a clear, definite sense of cultural nationalism at work" in Ellison's thinking that ought to be acknowledged.[48] Following in Neal's intellectual footsteps, Houston A. Baker Jr., before his most recent about-face, found that not only *Invisible Man* but also Ellison's essay "The Little Man at Chehaw Station" provide powerful supports for a neo–Black Aesthetic account of black literature and culture.[49]

Perhaps more telling than the capacity of Black Aesthetic sensibilities to accommodate Ellison's work is the way that even some of the most unsparing critics of the Black Arts movement, almost despite themselves, describe an Ellison who differs little from the portrait painted by Cruse, Neal, and Baker. Black Aestheticians made it their business to discover or re-create a black tradition—a tradition that not only traced a connection from one author to the next but imposed a responsibility on black writers to write from within the race. With respect to the first point, Ellison had explicitly rejected one version of black literary lineage in his celebrated exchange with critic Irving Howe. Howe's essay "Black Boys and Native Sons" had simply taken for granted a natural lineage connecting the old lion Richard Wright to the young cubs Ellison and James Baldwin, and on this basis had chastised the younger writers for failing to admit how much of their success depended on the aesthetic forays of the older writer. Ellison's sharp response—"Wright was no spiritual father of mine"—was elaborated in an often-quoted passage that sought to distinguish literary "relatives" from literary "ancestors." According to Ellison:

> While one can do nothing about choosing one's relatives, one can, as artist, choose one's "ancestors." Wright was, in this sense, a "relative," Hemingway an "ancestor." Langston Hughes, whose work I knew in grade school and whom I knew before I knew Wright, was a "relative"; Eliot, whom I was to meet only many years later, and Malraux and Dostoyevsky and Faulkner were "ancestors" if you please or don't please![50]

This is the sort of Ellisonian statement that riled Black Aestheticians with its acceptance of white writers as standards and influences. It is also the kind of statement that gave a critic like Henry Louis Gates Jr. some purchase in criticizing the inadequacy of the Black Arts program. Gates observed pointedly in the 1980s that it "is one of the ironies of the study of black literature that our critical activity is, almost by definition, a comparative one, since many of our writers seem to be as influenced by Western masters, writing in English as well as outside it, as they are by indigenous, Afro-American oral or even written forms."[51] The burden of practical application implied by this observation—as far as matters of teaching and anthologizing are concerned—seemed to portend integrated course syllabi and anthologies in which black and white canonical works from a variety of historical eras would press cheek to jowl with folktales, popular myths, and musical lyrics from an equally varied set of backgrounds. Yet the premise of a "comparative" enterprise is that one must first have discrete entities to place alongside one another, and Gates contended that the contours of the black literary tradition had yet to be effectively limned: "We shall, however, have to name the discrete seemingly disparate elements that compose the structures of which our vernacular literary traditions consist."[52]

So that while the direction of this new critical enterprise might have been incessantly toward a literary multiracialism, the immediate task was writing "a detailed account of the Afro-American literary tradition."[53] Gates's brief against Black Aestheticians, then, was not so much that they were preoccupied with the blackness of black literature, but that they were going about the task of accounting for it in the wrong way: " 'Blackness' is not a material object, an absolute, or an event, but a trope," Gates insisted, with the black writer acting as "the point of consciousness of his or her *language*. If the writer does embody a 'Black Aesthetic,' then it can be measured not by content but by a complex structure of meanings."[54] In the near term, then, despite Gates's acknowledgment of the black writer's multiracial heritage, Ellison would have to rest content with being more closely identified with his "relatives" than his chosen "ancestors." Thus Gates's *Norton Anthology of African American Literature*, in what may well become the definitive packaging of Ellison for the near future, places Ellison "in a chain of tradition that connects the slave narratives to autobiographical strategies employed a full century later in works such as Richard Wright's *Black Boy*, Claude Brown's *Manchild in the Promised Land*, Ralph Ellison's *Invisible Man*, and Toni Morrison's *Beloved.*"[55]

Ellison as transracialist. Ellison as race man. Ellison as high theorist. Ellison as folk artist. How are we to take these multiple guises? Jerry Watts has suggested that much of this multiplicity is merely apparent, a result of misreading. In Watts's estimation, "Ellison has often been misinterpreted by black nationalists as a kindred spirit. Insofar as he celebrates black folk culture, he appears sympathetic to a black cultural nationalism, but Ellison is not a black nationalist. He is a Negro nationalist and insofar as he believes that Negro culture is an American phenomenon and occupies a centrality within American culture, Ellison is an American nationalist."[56] And despite the many problems in Watts's reading of Ellison, there is something worth hanging on to in his conclusion. Ellison, for all his affinities with the role of race man, was in the final instance not entirely assimilable to black nationalism. Yet we would also err in concluding that his multiple guises are only misperceptions because what has made possible the contradictory appropriations of Ralph Ellison's work is that his writing so effectively rings the changes on black political and social life during the era of formal and explicit American racial segregation, stretching from the end of the nineteenth century until the mid-1960s. This period found a myriad of ways to cover the "Who Speaks for the Negro?" song, a tune that found elegant recapitulation in the narrator's final, haunting question in *Invisible Man*: "Who knows but that on the lower frequencies, I speak for you."[57]

If Ellison's work continues to resonate in our post-segregation era, it may be because notwithstanding the rather significant changes that the Civil Rights movement has wrought in American life generally, and in black American life more specifically, the key in which black politics has been played remains largely the same as it did prior to the modern Civil Rights and Black Power movements, when significant portions of black America existed outside of representational politics so that, to quote Adolph Reed, "the masses do not speak; someone speaks for them."[58]

What *Invisible Man* and the essays surrounding it can help bring into view is the way that the violent sweeping of black Americans from the political stage in the south at the end of the nineteenth century had the effect of sending the problem of inadequate black representation rumbling like a shock wave through the whole of American social and cultural life. Ellison was, of course, not the first or only observer of this shock. Yet largely because his critical and imaginative writings often acted as a corrosive splashed on the surface of what had appeared to be compelling representations of "the Negro," he was able to expose as tendentious distortions the apparent truths conveyed in these representations. But while Ellison was able to "see" this dynamic, he could not necessarily arrest it. That is, what his writing also demonstrated was that attempting to represent "the Negro" outside of the political realm of direct representation—whether one did so literarily, sociologically, philosophically, administratively, or philanthropically—was to enter a hall of mirrors, from which one was most likely to emerge with only misshapen images of oneself. *Invisible Man*'s troubled protagonist, who feels himself "surrounded by mirrors of hard, distorting glass," puts the matter quite memorably: "When [others] approach me they see only my surroundings, themselves, or figments of their imagination—indeed everything and anything except me" (3).

It is also crucial to keep in mind that although Ellison was attuned, as perhaps few others were, to the variety of ways that race shaped and refracted American reality, he necessarily approached the subjects of "race," "America," and "democracy" from a specific standpoint—that of the novelist—and as a result was as likely as any other commentator to assume that the lens provided by his medium was the one best suited to bring his subjects into view. The problem of race, then, was the problem of the novel.

Here Ellison was both wrong and right. Wrong, because the problem of race, as, to our dismay, conservative white southerners have recognized perhaps better than any other group, is at bottom a problem of politics and economics—of constitution making and of wielding power legislatively and economically in order to mobilize broad constituencies to preserve an unequal social order. And it is precisely in its representation of the political side of the American experience that the American novel, with some notable exceptions, has been notoriously weak. In the words of Ellison's sometimes-nemesis, Irving Howe, "Ideology is sometimes treated by the American novelists as if it were merely a form of private experience. Those massive political institutions, parties and movements which in the European novel occupy the space between the abstractions of ideology and the intimacies of personal life are barely present in America."[59]

But it is also for this very reason that Ellison was right. The institution of the American novel was so deeply implicated in redefining race in America away from the realm of political parties and movements and into the intimacies of personal life that Ellison's reflections on his craft could not help but cast light on the construction and reconstruction of the problem of the color line.

Confronting Ellison, then, means trying at once to see through the window on reality provided by the novel while also getting at what the novel as social practice necessarily obscures. Jerry G. Watts's *Heroism and the Black Intellectual* embraces the second half of this project, making a point not to engage in any critical reading of Ellison's *Invisible Man*, explaining that a "literary dialogue with *Invisible Man* is not pertinent to my study. Furthermore I claim no expertise in such matters." Watts, instead, elevates Ellison's "explicit social and political writings to a status they do not normally occupy in discussions of his ouvre [*sic*]."[60] What this line of analysis necessarily misses is that it was only because Ellison was a novelist that he was able to command our attention, and, somewhat even more ironically, that it was largely because he was identified with *one* novel that his critical and political writings could take the shape that they did.

In some respects, more remarkable than Ellison's inability to complete his second novel is the way his two volumes of published essays orbit tightly around *Invisible Man* without managing to be more synthetic than they are. Although Ellison works and reworks the question of the Negro's role in America and the responsibility of the novelist to the project of American democracy, his critical reflections remain occasional: transcripts of interviews; responses to attacks, both real and imagined; book, film, and music reviews. Rather than systematize his insights, Ellison allowed them to stand, sometimes contradictorily, alongside one another, a practice that made him in some sense the master of the occasion of criticism, turning a single instance into an X ray of the social organism infected by race at that historical moment.

When the occasion called for it, Ellison could highlight the moral evasiveness of Ernest Hemingway's modernist technique, complaining in "Twentieth-Century Fiction and the Black Mask of Humanity" that "Hemingway was alert only to Twain's technical discoveries—the flexible colloquial language, the sharp naturalism, the thematic potentialities of adolescence. Thus what for Twain was a means to a moral end became for Hemingway an end in itself." In this diagnosis, Hemingway finds himself "with no tragic mood indigenous to his society upon which he could erect a tragic art."[61] It is, however, a very different Hemingway that Ellison describes in his exchange with Irving Howe, in which he tries to distance himself from Richard Wright. Ellison's latter-day Hemingway is no stranger to the mode of tragedy, because "all that he wrote—and this is very important—was imbued with a spirit beyond the tragic with which I could feel at home, for it was very close to the feeling of the blues, which are, perhaps, as close as Americans can come to expressing the spirit of tragedy."[62]

Ellison does provide us means of explaining some of these contradictions. In a note prefacing the first publication of "Twentieth-Century Fiction and the Black Mask of Humanity," Ellison attributes the discrepancy between these assessments of Hemingway at least in part to his youthfulness:

> *When I started rewriting this essay it occurred to me that its value might be somewhat increased if it remained very much as I wrote it during 1946. For in that form it is what a young member of a*

> *minority felt about much of our writing. Thus I've left in much of*
> *the bias and short-sightedness, for it says perhaps as much about*
> *me as a member of a minority as it does about literature.* [63]

These were, then, the views held by a younger version of the writer, but
not those he would profess at a later date. The "truer" Ellison would be
the more mature version of the writer. To the degree, however, that Ellison attributes his bias and his shortsightedness not only to his youth
but to his status as a member of a racial minority, he suggests a critical attitude toward his writing in which each essay (and we might add
his novel here as well) constitutes a critical snapshot of the way that
ascribed racial status refracts and is refracted through some of the central issues of particular historical moments. Rather than resolve these
moments into a single, coherent image, it might be more effective, for
now, to allow an encounter with Ellison to be both an encounter with
those specific moments as well as with race as we live it in the present.
Looking at and through Ellison will be simultaneously a way of looking
at and through ourselves—although perhaps only for the time being.
Taking seriously Ellison's democratic hopes may be to imagine a world
in which *Invisible Man* no longer speaks immediately to us or for us as a
way of investigating contemporary American identity. As Ellison himself wrote, "It is our fate as human beings always to give up some good
things for other good things, to throw off certain bad circumstances only
to create others. Thus there is a value for the writer in trying to give as
thorough a report of social reality as possible. Only by doing so may we
grasp and convey the cost of change."[64] Such a task is what I hope to
continue here.

Ralph Ellison and the Cultural Turn in Black Politics

In proclaiming Miguel de Cervantes's *Don Quixote* "the most powerful weapon in the arsenal of the bourgeoisie in its war against feudalism and aristocracy," Czech critic Georgi Dimitrov celebrated Cervantes's novel for having "made the vestiges of chivalry the object of universal ridicule." The kernel of truth within Dimitrov's claim makes one want to forgive his hyperbole.[1] Part of the crucial, if sometimes ephemeral, political work that novels do is to transform noble and praiseworthy habits, beliefs, and actions into objects of scorn. A novel's satiric, parodic, and irreverent portraits, even when making up only a small part of a book's aesthetic agenda, can still account for its most striking political and social effects.[2]

How then to assess *Invisible Man* and its parodic treatment of white liberal philanthropists, black college presidents, and left-wing radicals? Would it be correct to paraphrase Dimitrov and declare Ellison's novel an indispensable weapon of the black bourgeoisie in its war against white racial paternalism? Or did other aesthetic forms prove more central to this cultural and social campaign?

This last question is, of course, a leading one, because it has long been asserted that music rather than literature has been the most politically powerful cultural force wielded by black Americans in the struggle against inequality. No matter how highly scholars have esteemed black novels, most critics of black culture insist that black popular music—whether spirituals, ragtime, blues, jazz, gospel, hip-hop, or rap—has been much more effective than the novel in challenging white societal norms. Langston Hughes argues in "The Negro Artist and the Racial Mountain" that the blues of Bessie Smith offered the black artist a weapon against mediocre white bourgeois standards: "Let the blare of Negro jazz bands and the bellowing voice of Bessie Smith singing Blues penetrate the closed ears of the colored near-intellectuals until they listen and perhaps understand."[3] Writers—poets and novelists alike—would do well to emulate musicians and singers. If *Invisible Man* has been at all successful in helping to undermine the authority of white paternalism, it presumably has done so not by marshaling the stylistic resources of novelistic form but rather by appropriating the resources of black musical culture. "*Invisible Man* is a jazz text," asserts Horace Porter in his critical study of Ellison's relation to black music, while other critics stress the blues as Ellison's preferred musical idiom.[4] Houston Baker has argued that Ellison "derives his most forceful examples from the vernacular: Blues seem implicitly to comprise the *All* of American culture."[5]

In accounts like those offered by Baker, the story of the cultural triumph of black music turns out to be a story of political triumph for the black rank and file. The trumping of novelistic tradition by oral and musical forms marked, according to Hazel Carby, "the historical moment of the failure of the black bourgeoisie to achieve cultural hegemony and to become a dominant social force."[6] We are not, in Carby's account, to lament this failure, but on the contrary, to see it as signaling the successes of black working-class resistance to the designs of their would-be middle-class mentors: black migrant women thwarting the efforts of club women and the Urban League "to police and discipline the[ir] behavior,"[7] or the capacity of young zoot-suiters to contest "the class-conscious, integrationist attitudes of middle-class blacks."[8] Black middle-class failure would appear to have set the political stage for black working-class success. What complicates this picture of successful working-class cultural insurgency, however, is that it is not quite true. Black middle-class legitimacy has not rested primarily on its success in disciplining the social, moral, and aesthetic behaviors and tastes of a black peasantry and working class. On the contrary, some degree of lower-class unruliness and unaccountability ("Why do they act the way they do?") has tended to work in favor of aspiring black spokespersons in their battle with well-meaning whites for the right to speak on behalf of black America. Although black elites have been sincere in their desire to "uplift" the race, the most visible measure of their success has not been the triumph of so-called bourgeois values among the nonprofessional laboring classes but rather the substitution of black professionals, managers, and intellectuals for their white counterparts within those institutions charged with administering to the needs of black populations. The sought-for prize has been managerial authority over the nation's Negro problem. Indeed, so apparently successful was this strategy that as early as 1940, W. E. B. Du Bois declared, "No longer was it possible or thinkable anywhere in the United States to study and discuss the Negro without letting him speak for himself and without having that speaking done by a well-equipped person, if such person was wanted."[9] By Du Bois's reckoning, the Talented Tenth, the small stratum of college-educated Negroes dedicated to racial service, had been granted crucial recognition to speak in matters pertaining to the race.

This recognition was, however, not necessarily acknowledged by its putative beneficiaries, and when such recognition was refused, culture was not the only or even the primary ground of contestation. Despite the common difficulties created by racial discrimination, the differences in the given interests of blacks at varying socioeconomic levels and in different regions could produce competing political and organizational imperatives. To illustrate, Du Bois's famous January 1934 *Crisis* editorial, "Segregation," clearly scandalized the upper echelon of black and white race liberals by announcing, "The thinking colored people of the United States must stop being stampeded by the word segregation."[10] Coming from the house organ of the NAACP, the nation's most visible Civil Rights organization, Du Bois expected that his words would shock and offend the Talented Tenth, but he also assumed they would find attentive listeners at the lower rungs of the socioeconomic order. Accordingly, he described himself (and most subsequent scholars have echoed this description) as eschewing the intelligentsia in favor of the black masses. He wrote, "The upper class Negro has almost never been nationalistic. He has never planned or thought of a Negro state or a Negro church or a Negro school. This solution has always been a thought upsurging from the mass."[11]

Yet even as Du Bois urged his black readers to focus on building within the race, black tenant farmers in Arkansas were establishing an interracial Southern Tenant Farmer's Union to press their demands.[12]

And at about the same time, George Streator, who assisted Du Bois for a time at *Crisis*, left the magazine to organize black and white workers with the Amalgamated Clothing Workers of America in New York and Norfolk, Virginia. The point here is not that the program Du Bois announced in the pages of *Crisis* in 1934 led him to oppose these interracial efforts,[13] but that the position he described as sanctioned by the desires of the black masses was not even at that moment universally reflective of their actions.

Almost as if to shore up the uncertain mandate he claimed had been granted him by the rank and file for his pragmatic response to what he saw as the persistence of segregation for the foreseeable future, Du Bois adduced the cultivation of black culture as a model for economic organization. He wrote, "I proposed that in economic lines, just as in lines of literature and religion, segregation should be planned and organized and carefully thought through."[14] And to wrap up his case, Du Bois demanded that the NAACP board of directors declare whether or not they believed "in Negro history, Negro literature and art, in business or in Negro spirituals."[15]

Although such writers as Hughes, Carby, and Paul Gilroy have stressed musical culture as an indispensable tool in the working class's effort to overturn bourgeois leadership, Du Bois's political tussles suggest another function for black cultural forms. In conflicts between and among intellectual elites, the act of aligning oneself with the putatively distinct and relatively autonomous cultural styles emerging from "below" has been brandished as if this alignment guaranteed a proxy from the working class even when no power had actually been ceded to black laborers. So that although Du Bois called for "tactical segregation," ostensibly on behalf of the black masses whom he enjoined to "evolve and support your own social institutions," he had not in truth dispensed with the idea of elite leadership.[16] Nor had his many critics. For it has been the so-called Talented Tenth, beginning with the establishment of the Fisk Jubilee singers in the middle of the nineteenth century and continuing with greater urgency during the Harlem Renaissance, that has linked black political success to the production of a black culture that would include "the emergence of a distinct and credible Negro literature."[17] So, if over the last several decades of the twentieth century we have come to take as given the claim that black cultural production is necessarily central to black politics, it seems arguable that what we have seen is the success of, rather than the failure of, a bourgeois hegemonic project centered in an African American politics of culture.

This politics of culture began to take shape in the wake of the collapse of congressional Reconstruction of the south and in varying ways has extended into the present moment, enveloping the Black Aesthetic movement, black literary feminisms, Afrocentrisms, academic vernacular critiques, cultural studies, or transatlantic critiques. What this project entailed, quite simply, was pointing out the failure of available modes of representation to transmit the needs and desires of black populations, and then proffering in their stead a more adequate means of representation, a "speaking for you" that presumably does not falsify or distort the subject represented. This problem finds its roots in the political defeat that ended Reconstruction and that for Ellison formed the ground for understanding the United States during the first half of the twentieth century. Throughout his career, Ellison would continually refer to the end of Reconstruction as historically pivotal. Writing in 1945, he insisted, "Since 1876 the race issue has been like a stave driven into the American system of values."[18] And giving testimony before a Senate committee in 1966, where he labeled the "squashing of Reconstruction" as "a political disaster," Ellison drew the Senate's attention to the fact "that during the end of Reconstruction there was mass violence against Negroes who were functioning in legislatures." He pointed out: "In Louisiana, for instance, none of the white legislators appeared at a meeting. The Negroes did appear, and were all killed by the Police Department. This is American history, and it has been kept from us."[19] That this erasure has been effective is beyond doubt—how many school-aged children (or college students, for that matter), black or white, can name any of the black legislators who served in Congress during the Reconstruction era? This ignorance is only part of the problem, however. More troubling is the way white supremacy's violent expulsion of black representation from national and state assemblies and the accompanying rewriting of state laws and constitutions during the 1890s have been subtly if inadvertently naturalized by subsequent "black" political projects in the sphere of culture.[20]

Sixty years before the publication of Ralph Ellison's *Invisible Man*, Anna Julia Cooper's *A Voice from the South* (1892) made the following observation:

A conference of earnest Christian men have met at regular inter-
vals for some years past to discuss the best methods of promoting
the welfare and development of colored people in this country.
Yet, strange as it may seem, they have never invited a colored
man or even intimated that one would be welcome to take part
in their deliberations.[21]

In making this observation, Cooper was doing two things. First, she
was contesting an Episcopal clergyman's claim that the Episcopalian
style of worship was "not adapted to the rude untutored minds of the
Freedmen" who would be better served by "the Methodists and Bap-
tists whither their racial proclivities undeniably tend."[22] In response,
Cooper pointed out that this presumption of incompatibility between
blacks and Episcopalians was nothing more than a way of justifying and
camouflaging the fact that blacks had already been excluded from the
church's councils.

Cooper's second goal was to draw attention to the oddity of all-white
assemblies presuming to deliberate over the needs of black Americans.
Of course, Cooper knew quite well that in the eyes of most of her readers, there was nothing strange or unusual in such an assembly taking
upon itself the responsibility of making decisions on behalf of black
people. Indeed, it was only during the all too brief moment of the Reconstruction era that blacks had been included in various legislative
delegations of the south. Given the north's abandonment of Reconstruction, along with the purging of black members from southern legislatures and the codification of Jim Crow laws throughout the south,
Cooper could not have doubted that the nation as a whole had come to
regard the *interracial* spectacle of Reconstruction and not the all-white
spectacle of the "redeemed" southern governments as strange, or, to use
Thomas Dixon Jr.'s word from his novel *The Clansman*, "remarkable."[23]

Against this bleak political backdrop, it is easy to see why Cooper's
project at bottom became an aesthetic one. As white reaction in the
1880s and 1890s further insulated state and national assemblies from
direct black political action, the task that fell to individuals like Cooper
was that of criticizing recurrent attempts by whites, like those in the
church assembly mentioned above, to represent and to deliberate on
the fate of black people without having first consulted black voices.
With no likelihood of integrating the state's deliberative assemblies,

Cooper's only hope was to bring to bear the force of religion and literature in an effort to influence moral attitudes.

To be sure, Cooper had no intention of abandoning the causes of suffrage and office holding. She specifically drew attention to the role that black women had played and were playing in keeping black men solidly within the ranks of the Republican Party. Yet nestled in the center of *A Voice from the South* is an extensive chapter of literary criticism in which Cooper severely censures the efforts of well-meaning white writers—most prominently Albion Tourgée, George Washington Cable, and William Dean Howells—to render accurately and sympathetically black characters. Even here Cooper proceeded more indirectly than directly, favoring aesthetics over moral rectitude, as indicated by her preference for writers "in whom the artistic or poetic instinct is uppermost" over "writers with a purpose or a lesson."[24] Her "political" aim was to go beyond doctrine and principle into an aestheticized realm where exclusively white efforts to represent blacks could be made to look and feel wrong—as if they were errors in critical judgment or taste—both to her readers and to the white authors of those representations.

Decades later, writing in the considerable cultural wake created by *Invisible Man*, leftist literary critic Kenneth Burke confided to Ellison that "you could and did get us to look for traces of unconscious Nortonism in our thinking," suggesting that among the effects of Ellison's *Invisible Man* was that of precipitating self-reflection or self-examination in well-intentioned white allies.[25] While in truth "Nortonism"—the social disease exemplified in the novel by the hapless white benefactor, Mr. Norton, as the tendency of allies to project their individual pathologies onto blacks under the guise of helping them—could afflict blacks as well as whites, Burke's quietly expressed self-examination indicates that Ellison in some small way had accomplished what Cooper had intended: he had reversed the critical gaze and (at least in Burke's case) had rendered white presumption about its insight into the ways of black people remarkable.

But Ellison did not initially assume that Negro culture was the best weapon to use in an assault on racial inequality. During the Great Depression, the possibility of and necessity for blacks to engage in direct political action had briefly challenged the ascendancy in elite circles of the indirect cultural politics characterized by both Cooper's aesthetic turn in the 1890s and the leadership of Charles S. Johnson during the period of the Harlem Renaissance in the 1920s when Johnson pushed Negro art and culture to the center of the political stage as the best means of changing American society.[26] The realities of the depression era prompted the young Ellison to declare it was not literature but political organizing that held out the most promise for changing American society. His report on the Third National Negro Congress, published in *New Masses* in May 1940 as "A Congress Jim Crow Didn't Attend," celebrates the transformative power of political action. Ellison describes one of the delegates, Hank Morgan, "a CIO organizer from the Chicago region," as a man "*transformed.*" When Morgan "spoke, all the violence that America has made our Negro heritage was flowing from him transformed into a will to change a civilization." Confessing himself to have been deeply affected by the delegates' approval of a resolution to join the CIO, Ellison writes, "And there in the faces of my people I saw strength. There with the whites in the audience I saw the positive forces of civilization and the best guarantee of America's future."[27]

According to Barbara Foley, Ellison's views on the Negro Congress were of a piece with much of the journalism he published during his intellectual apprenticeship in New York in the 1930s and 1940s, a time during which he "quite vigorously endorsed and supported the program and outlook of the U.S. Communist left."[28] Marxist thought remained influential in Ellison's thinking as late as 1944 when in a review of Gunnar Myrdal's *An American Dilemma* he decries how Booker T. Washington's "'Tuskegee Machine' served to deflect Negro energy away from direct political action."[29] Even this essay, however, registers what Michel Fabre has called a "change in emphasis" for Ellison—a move "from the narrowly political and economic toward the cultural."[30] Increasingly frustrated with both the Left and the Right, Ellison used the occasion of his Myrdal review to attack the tendency at both ends of the political spectrum to see "Negro culture and personality simply as the product of a 'social pathology.'" By the end of the essay, Ellison is treating societal transformation as a matter more cultural than political, proclaiming, "In Negro culture there is much of value for America as a whole. What is needed are Negroes to take it and create of it 'the uncreated consciousness of their race.' In doing so they will do far more; they will help create a more human American."[31] For his part, Ellison turned to the novel that became *Invisible Man.*

Published some eight years after the Myrdal review, *Invisible Man* might, then, be expected to constitute an unambiguous endorsement of the idea that cultural creation is essential to societal transformation. Yet this is not the case. Barbara Foley's forthcoming "From Communism to Brotherhood: The Drafts of *Invisible Man*" argues for significant Communist Party holdovers in the text of the novel.[32] The novel's historical commitment tends to preserve some of Ellison's earlier awareness that the means one chooses to fight inequality are determined in large part by one's specific historical moment. This awareness surfaces in the protagonist's grandfather's oft-quoted confession to his grandson: "I never told you, but our life is a war and I have been a traitor all my born days, a spy in the enemy's country ever since I give up my gun back in the Reconstruction" (16). This sentence economically references three distinct historical moments, the first being the armed struggle during the Civil War; the second marking the failed direct political struggle of the Reconstruction era; and the third indicating the period of "everyday" politics of resistance manifested in life, language, and behavior that gets adopted when the risks of engaging in more direct resistance are too high. This "third" moment corresponds to the period that historian Rayford Logan has called the nadir of African American history—the period extending from the 1890s through the turn of the century that was characterized by lynchings, race riots, the *Plessy* decision, broad-scale disfranchisement, convict labor, and Booker T. Washingtonian accommodationism.[33]

Because some of the resistance strategies adopted during the nadir recapitulated the strategies of everyday resistance employed under slavery, it is this third moment that has proved quite problematic in intellectual and cultural commentary about black life and politics. Scholars have been inclined to treat any recurrence as evidence that the truth about black political hopes and desires lies hidden within apparently nonpolitical activities. These studies, though historical in intent, tend to freeze and generalize specific moments in the historical experiences of black people, and then to read the whole of that history through the lens of this crystallization. Slavery—whether through its economics, its conditions of literacy, or its strategies of gendering black populations— provides the template for discussing black cultural production. The scholarship of Henry Louis Gates, Houston Baker, Hortense Spillers, and Paul Gilroy displays an "underlying commitment to a deductive style of *a priori* reasoning [that] seems to entail that critical distinctions and value judgements concerning black art have a *once-and-for-all-time* quality."[34] In all of these texts, something like "the memory of slavery," or an "economics of slavery" arising from specific historical experience, becomes a permanent fixture in the psyches of black people.

In Gilroy's view, then, it becomes possible to assert that for "the descendants of slaves, work signifies only servitude, misery, and subordination. Artistic expression, expanded beyond recognition from the grudging gifts offered by the masters as a token substitute for freedom from bondage, therefore becomes the means towards both individual self-fashioning and communal liberation."[35] This historical a priori absolves him from having to attend to broad range of activities undertaken by actual people in actual places. For example, Julie Saville's work has demonstrated that black laborers during the Reconstruction era in South Carolina did not simply eschew manual labor as a badge of slavery but insisted on "their right to work when, how and for whom they pleased and through these efforts to gain control over their labor fashioned a vision of democratic fulfillment."[36] Nor does recent historical study support Gilroy's contention that blacks during the era of emancipation assumed their most profound politics was necessarily transmitted "on a lower frequency where it is played, danced, and acted, as well as sung and sung about, because words, even words stretched by melisma and supplemented or mutated by the screams which still index the conspicuous power of the slave sublime, will never be enough to communicate its unsayable claims to truth."[37] Again, to quote Saville, "Written expression played a surprisingly significant role during the organization of public life of what was still a predominantly illiterate population. . . . The organized public life of freedpeople on the sea islands early linked written expression to the strength of a popular movement by adapting writing and reading to social processes by which the written word could provide even the illiterate with information and a means of collective expression."[38] In addition, the political activity of blacks in state conventions after emancipation revealed, in the words of Eric Foner, that a "central preoccupation . . . was equality before the law and suffrage." These desires were so remarkable that Foner goes on to comment, "Rarely has a community invested so many hopes in politics as blacks during Radical Reconstruction."[39] During these years, the radicalization of black political thought was as likely, if not more likely, to occur in open struggle as in what Gilroy terms the "partially hidden public sphere."[40]

It is not that these open struggles approached anywhere near the success that their proponents would have liked. Nothing close to the 1906 Niagara Movement's demand that the "Fourteenth Amendment [be] carried out to the letter and every State disfranchised in Congress which attempts to disfranchise its rightful voters" was ever realized over the first half of the twentieth century.[41] But it is heuristically useful to entertain the idea that if such movements had succeeded, the story of black cultural expression during the post-emancipation era would likely have unfolded differently. Certainly the literature of uplift that gathered momentum during the 1890s might have been drastically re-figured, as would some of the assumptions that inaugurated the Harlem Renaissance—both moments spawned literary schools that took for granted the expectation that unelected elites would speak and act on behalf of blacks generally. The goal of this sort of heuristic exercise, however, is not really to imagine how such a literature might have looked otherwise, but to read and hear existing objects of black cultural expression with an ear attuned to their own self-contradictory shadows and whispers, the muttering that says, "*But for the persistence of very injustices that I decry, I would not be standing before you.*" No such reminder is needed for the literature that is explicitly engaged in political and social protest—the literature that wears its historical contingency on its sleeve. Rather, the argument here is angled toward that literature—fictive and critical—that imagines its own relative autonomy from circumstances, the literature that imagines for itself the career of the classic.

The strange text that is James Weldon Johnson's 1912 *Autobiography of an Ex-Coloured Man* helps make this point. By putting forward black cultural achievement in the form of ragtime music, spirituals, the cake-walk, and the sermon as overwhelming evidence for black humanity and a powerful argument for black equality, *Ex-Coloured Man* exemplifies the cultural turn of the post-emancipation era as Johnson's protagonist seeks to realize the idea that by producing a classic black music, he might participate in the larger struggle for racial equality. Paradoxically, more illustrative than the case that Johnson's novel makes for culture is the case that it proves itself unable to make for the classic possibilities lying within black culture. That is, Johnson's novel reveals itself as a text that was written only because the quest to create a text of "classic" expression had to be abandoned along the way.

A novel masquerading as an autobiography, *Ex-Coloured Man* introduces itself as a story divulging a great secret—the narrator, who has lived most of his adult life as a white man, confesses that he is really black. The details of Johnson's novel are well known and only need to be mentioned briefly here: A young, musically talented boy spends his early youth in the north with his mother, believing that both of them are white until, one day, the school principal asks that all the white students stand. The narrator, who has risen with the white students, is told, however, to sit down. The discovery that he is classified as black takes the narrator on a course where he will presumably learn what it means to be a Negro. His new life becomes a somewhat picaresque journey through the American south, New York City, and, for a time, Europe. Facilitating his journey are the narrator's considerable musical skills, which enable him to become an accomplished ragtime pianist and which, while he is in Europe, help him conceive a life mission. He writes:

> I had been turning classic music into rag-time, a comparatively easy task; and this man had taken rag-time and made it classic. The thought came across me like a flash—It can be done, why can't I do it? From that moment my mind was made up. I clearly saw the way of carrying out the ambition I had formed when a boy.[42]

That ambition had been to become "a great man, a great coloured man, to reflect credit on the race and gain fame for myself." Accordingly, the narrator abandons his white benefactor in Europe and returns to the south to collect "themes and melodies . . . trying to catch the spirit of the Negro in his relatively primitive state."[43] He aborts this mission, however, after he stumbles onto a brutal lynching, and in response moves north, where he lives as a moderately successful white businessman who marries a white woman and has two children who do not know the truth of their origins.

When he begins his narration, the ex-colored man describes his decision to reveal that he is a Negro as a dangerous act. "Criminal," "playing with fire," "savage and diabolical" are some of the terms that he associates with his confessional desires. And yet by the end of the novel, he leaves us with the possibility that his earth-shaking revelation may have been no revelation at all, admitting, "Sometimes it seems to me that I have never really been a Negro, that I have been only a privileged spectator of their inner life." That his story may in the final instance divulge no secrets whatsoever (he does not, after all, even tell us his name) indicates that the feeling emphasized in the opening paragraph, the feeling of danger that comes from the possibility of being discovered, is not the novel's primary mood. Rather, the sentiment that prompts the narrator to tell his tale, the emotion "from which [he is] seeking relief," is "a vague feeling of unsatisfaction, of regret, of almost remorse." Directing us to the final paragraph of the novel, the narrator focuses this feeling of remorse on the remaining evidence of the road his life did not take after the lynching—the "little box in which I still keep my fast yellowing manuscripts the only tangible remnants of a vanished dream, a dead ambition, a sacrificed talent."[44] These yellowing manuscripts are the notes toward a work of classic expression that did not get written. In its place we have Johnson's novel, a story haunted by the narrator's never-attempted composition. In seeking relief from his troublesome feelings, the narrator has proffered his readers a trade, asking that we accept the story of his life in place of the promised classic.

Reading Johnson's *The Autobiography of an Ex-Coloured Man* as an elaboration of the tension between the story that does get written and the classic composition that is never realized suggests a critical heuristic for approaching the corpus of twentieth-century American literature on black-white racial difference—a literature that can be read as a concatenation of those texts that did manage to get written in lieu of the classics that did not. On this view, the success of twentieth-century American literature can never escape the shadow of its failure, an argument that Ellison made in such pieces as "Twentieth-Century Fiction and the Black Mask of Humanity." Here he insists that in evading the moral problem presented by the Negro, twentieth-century American writers had evaded the very thing that could have enabled them to equal "Mark Twain's great classic, *Huckleberry Finn*."[45] America's twentieth-century literary masterpieces stand dwarfed against the faint background of what they otherwise might have been—a truly classic literature. Marred by this failure despite its technical brilliance, twentieth-century American literature argued eloquently for the idea that a better society might produce a better literature.

Ellison made the strong version of this argument only intermittently throughout his literary life. And even as he made it, he undercut its utopian thrust by applying as a standard of measure nineteenth-century American literature, which had been written in a society less free than the one in which Ellison lived. As a result, his argument that a better society might produce a better literature was often supplanted by the insistence that a literature that took seriously the moral problem of the Negro could, like the Declaration of Independence and the U.S. Constitution, be better than the society that had produced it. Even so, the whole of Ellison's intellectual career was an ongoing investigation into the possibilities of American expression, an investigation that required freeing the Negro from the representational shackles of paternalism that had been applied after emancipation.

As a novel, *Invisible Man* specifically uncouples the problem of slavery and the problem of emancipation. Speaking about his grandfather, the invisible man observes that his formerly enslaved ancestor "never had any doubts about his humanity—that was left to his 'free' offspring" (580). The problems of the enslaved and the problems of their free descendants, though related, were different. In the wake of the failure of Reconstruction, various nongovernmental bodies, commissions, philanthropic organizations, and social science professionals and scholars were charged, by constitutional and legislative default, with the task of administering the lives of black people. Accountable to no one but themselves, these experts on "the Negro problem" were readily granted authority to speak on behalf of blacks to white governments eager to "solve" that problem and get on with the business of governing.

Mr. Norton, a founder and trustee of the Negro college attended by the invisible man, delineates this structure of administration. A "Bostonian, smoker of cigars, teller of polite Negro stories, shrewd banker, skilled scientist, director, philanthropist, forty years a bearer of the white man's burden, and for sixty a symbol of the Great Traditions" (37), Norton is an anthology of white administrative and discursive control over black populations: moral, social, economic, scientific, institutional, and cultural. These discourses define a grid, presumably rational and benevolent, enabling an accounting for the lives and personalities of black people. What Ellison illustrates by confronting Norton with Trueblood and the denizens of the Golden Day is not only the inability of that grid to predict and account for the people that Norton meets, but also the irrationality and pathology that motivates Norton's philanthropic relationship to black populations. Norton's incestuous desires for his own daughter, which are drawn out in his discussion with the sharecropper Jim Trueblood, underscore the point that Ellison makes in *Shadow and Act* when he writes, "Philanthropy on the psychological level is often guilt-motivated."[46]

Although Kenneth Burke's admission to unconscious Nortonism attests to the effectiveness of Ellison's portraiture for at least one reader, it would be overstating the case to say that through such representations *Invisible Man* made the vestiges of white paternalism obsolete; paternalism remained a force throughout Ellison's life and into the present. Yet Ellison's career did mark a heightened vulnerability of white liberals and leftists to questions about the psychological motivations of their political allegiances to blacks. And with the coming of the modern Civil Rights movement, there was also a partial shifting of the race problem away from the private philanthropic sector, represented by the Carnegie Foundation's underwriting of the research that gave us Gunnar Myrdal's *An American Dilemma*, back toward the political realm where the problem of race was again presumed amenable to activism, organizing, legislation, executive orders, and vigorous enforcement of the laws.

The racial dimension of this shift can be gauged by contrasting Ellison's National Book Award–winning novel with its most visible predecessor, Richard Wright's acclaimed *Native Son*: in 1940 when Wright's novel appeared, it still seemed aesthetically defensible for a black author to give over the articulation of the Negro's plight to a white character, Max, who as Bigger Thomas's lawyer is allowed to speak authoritatively on the black condition. Max's views are not endorsed unambiguously by the novel, but they are not treated with the heavy irony that attends the attempts of characters—Mr. Norton, the young Mr. Emerson, and Brother Jack—to speak on behalf of the Negro in *Invisible Man*. Certainly the broader literary and political culture in the United States in the 1950s continued to produce representations of whites speaking presumably sympathetically and authoritatively about black character and conditions, but Ellison's rebuke of Irving Howe's remarks on black writers in "Black Boys and Native Sons" as well as the storms of controversy that met the Moynihan Report and the publication of William Styron's *The Confessions of Nat Turner* in the 1960s were unambiguous indications that white representation of black consciousness was on the defensive and would continue to be challenged by Ellison as well as by those who criticized him among the Black Arts movement.

Yet even though the differences in the conclusions of *Native Son* and *Invisible Man* help point to the shift from white to black authoritative voices, the difference is more a matter of degree than kind. What enables Bigger Thomas to appear to slip the dragnet of Max's political theory is not so much an alternative politics as a statement of identity: "'I didn't want to kill!' Bigger shouted. 'But what I killed for, I *am*!'" And against this assertion, Max's despairing "No; no; no. . . . Bigger, not that"[47] can be of only limited effect. Likewise the whole of *Invisible Man* could be described as a tortured assertion of an identity that has not yet assumed, and might possibly never assume, a form adequate to its voice. What the narrator claims himself to be, he is.

Native Son certainly did not give any indication that culture could provide the matrix of complexity that politics and sociology could not quite account for, but the space that is Bigger was waiting to be filled in by something other than violence. There was plenty yet left for culture to do.

The stinging portraits of Mr. Norton and Brother Jack seemed to augur well for the assault on white paternalism. The segregation of blacks from whites in American society meant that even if critics took exception to Ellison's less than charitable characterizations of well-meaning white characters, it was difficult to refute the charge that whites did not know blacks as well as they thought they did. Authority over the Negro was continuing its move from outside to "inside"—toward those who could claim themselves "flesh of the flesh and bone of the bone of those who reside within the veil."[48] What would be less easy to counter, however, in a world defined by inadequate black political representation would be the paternalism of those who presumed to speak on behalf of the race from within the race, and who could claim on the basis of their identities to know whereof they spoke: the Bledsoes, the Barbees, the Rases, and the Mary Rambos. Claims to represent the needs and desires of the race emanating from the experiences represented by characters like these could not be discounted on the basis of a lack of knowledge. What Ellison had hoped to accomplish in *Invisible Man* was an assertion of identity that could, through expressing the ideals of a democratic society, remain at once cultural and political. This task threw him squarely into the problem of representation, a problem that is the subject of the next chapter.

CHAPTER 2

Race, Literature, and the Politics of Numbers, or Not Quite a Million Men Marching

The death of Tod Clifton at the hands of a police officer prompts *Invisible Man*'s protagonist to stage Clifton's funeral as a public Harlem-wide event honoring Brother Tod as a fallen hero. Clifton, who had been a stalwart member of the Brotherhood, is gunned down after having bolted the organization's ranks to transform himself into a street vendor peddling dancing Sambo puppets that can be made to perform obscene dances on cue. The puppets are offensive, but their meaning is clear: Clifton, the invisible man, and all of Harlem are being made to dance to the tune of a variety of manipulators. Troubled as always by symbols whose meaning seem just beyond his grasp, the invisible man cannot simply write Clifton off as an apostate to the cause of true brotherhood. And upon seeing the anger on the street following the murder of another young man, the protagonist seizes the opportunity to make a collective statement. The result of his efforts is an enigma—an enigma created by the spectacle of, shall we say, not quite a million men marching. For the protagonist appears to have taken the measure of the street correctly. The people come out in droves for the funeral procession, where the invisible man stands "at the head with the old community leaders" looking back on the assemblage he has helped to create. Seeing this spectacle, he wonders at the motives of the various participants:

It was a slow march and as I looked back from time to time I could see young zoot-suiters, hep cats, and men in overalls and poolhall gamblers stepping into the procession. Men came out of barber shops with lathered faces, their neckcloths hanging to watch and comment in hushed voices. And I wondered, Are they all Clifton's friends, or is it just for the spectacle, the slow-paced music? (450–51)

Then as the "crowds approached the park from all directions," the protagonist finds himself pondering further:

Why were they here? Why had they found us? Because they knew Clifton? Or for the occasion his death gave them to express their protestations, a time and place to come together, to stand touching and sweating and breathing and looking in a common direction? Was either explanation adequate in itself? Did it signify love or politicized hate? And could politics ever be an expression of love? (452)

This series of questions, which will be taken up momentarily, suggests that the protagonist's apparent mastery of getting the people to turn out yields at best only partial insight into the motives of the marchers. He cannot be sure what their participation means, an uncertainty that is not surprising in this novel whose protagonist is always only dimly aware of the full implications of his actions. And yet from another angle, the protagonist's consternation may be only apparent. When disciplined by Brother Jack and the Brotherhood for having staged a hero's funeral for a man they consider to be "a traitorous merchant of vile instruments of anti-Negro, anti-minority racist bigotry" (466), the protagonist insists suddenly that he does indeed know the minds of the people who turned out for the funeral, asserting that "the political consciousness of Harlem is exactly a thing I know something about" (471). He then proceeds to point out that he has succeeded where his leftist colleagues have failed—that is, in organizing a large-scale event that worked "because we gave them the opportunity to express their feelings, to affirm themselves" (469).

Yet even here the invisible man's warrant for this claim seems dubious. In the narrative's account of the funeral, only he and a preacher actually speak, the latter to read some Scripture from the Bible. As for the mass assembly, though, the people are there primarily in their physicality—"The crowd sweated and throbbed, and though it was silent, there were many things directed toward me through its eyes"; "the crowd boiled, sweated, heaved" (459–60). The message spoken through the collective eyes of the crowd manifests as a palpable emotional and physical tension. But precisely what the crowd means to express and affirm remains largely a matter of interpretation.

The slippage between event and motivation, event and organizer, emotion and expression, as well as cause and effect in Ellison's representation of Tod Clifton's funeral seems eerily prescient in the light of the discussions surrounding Louis Farrakhan's 1995 Million Man March, an event that was supposed to inaugurate a new era in black political life in the closing years of the twentieth century. Louis Farrakhan, head of the Nation of Islam—but bidding to become the nation's preeminent black leader—had proclaimed October 16 of the year a day of atonement and called for a million black men to assemble on the Mall in Washington D.C. to make history. As everyone knew, the Nation of Islam's politics were conservative and patriarchal. And in keeping with this politics, Farrakhan had insisted that renewal of the black population had to begin with men. Yet what was striking about the march was the way it appealed to many activists on the Left, many who boasted of their feminist credentials. So that even as the march's historical importance was being proclaimed, questions about its fundamental meaning—Why were they marching? What were the march's politics?—remained very much in the air.

To account for *Invisible Man*'s prescience regarding an event that Ellison could not have foreseen, we need look no further than the march's reliance on a problem of representation as its organizing principle. Ellison knew that administering "the Negro problem" in the twentieth century had depended heavily on claims of the representational and theoretical accuracy from "on high" or from "outside" the race, and that a cultural politics of representation involved exposing these claims as inadequate to the reality of "race" in black American life and politics. Farrakhan's "Day of Atonement" offered itself up as both a corroboration of and a challenge to commonly held images of black men. By coming to the Washington Mall, the marchers were supposed to demonstrate that black men were not the monsters commonly portrayed in the media, even as they atoned for presumed shortcomings as fathers, husbands, sons, and brothers. America had not accurately seen black men.

Correcting misperceptions about the minds and capacities of black America was the project held in common by Ellison's novel and Farrakhan's march. When Brother Tobitt in *Invisible Man* questions the protagonist's claim to knowing something about the people of Harlem, the invisible man responds:

> I've worked among the people up here. Ask your wife to take you around to the gin mills and the barber shops and the juke joints and the churches, Brother. Yes, and the beauty parlors on Saturdays when they're frying hair. (471)

In the invisible man's estimation, this unrecorded history critiques the official recorded histories, and as such challenges the truth of official views. Authority in this instance devolves upon those who have seen or lived the "part of reality which the committee seems to have missed" (472)—those who have seen the previously unseen, and whose knowledge, if taken into account, might helpfully redirect the course of those who presume to lead or represent. In similar fashion, Farrakhan's marchers were to take the true image of black men from the realms of everyday life where it had been obscured, into the clean, bright light of the national and international media.

Yet however justified the invisible man's rebuke of the committee may be, his view of the world is not fully vindicated at this point in the novel. As compelling as his criticism is, he still fails to see until the last minute the part of reality represented by Jack's artificial eye. If everyone is partially blind, then no one sees particularly well. How can one then assume the accuracy of the words spoken in gin mills, beauty parlors, and juke joints? Is there a protocol that must be invoked when accounts "on the ground" differ?

Obviously Brother Jack's solution—"We do not shape our policies to the mistaken and infantile notions of the man in the street. Our job is not to *ask* them what they think but to *tell* them!"—is not the answer (473). Indeed, perhaps no other statement in the novel so effectively unmasks the anti-democratic anti-egalitarianism of the Brotherhood. But is Brother Jack entirely out of line in suggesting that the man in the street just might be mistaken on some points, points at which the distant analyst might be better informed?

On this score, it helps to remember that well before the staging of Clifton's funeral, the novel has already demonstrated its skepticism about the effectiveness of rooting one's identity entirely in the quotidian realities of one's lived experience. After having overcome his embarrassment over eating yams (he had initially wanted to shed his rural, provincial past for a sophisticated, cosmopolitan, and politically up-to-date identity), the narrator defiantly and openly purchases several more sweet potatoes from the street vendor while asserting with glee, "They're my birthmark. . . . I yam what I yam" (266). This glee is short-lived, however. The protagonist's ingestion of the savory tautology of self-identity is interrupted when "an unpleasant taste bloomed in my mouth now as I bit the end of the yam and threw it into the street; it had been frostbitten" (267).

In many respects, Ellison's protagonist operates in a role similar to that of Gramsci's "organic intellectual," that is, as an agent who "neither sentimentally acquiesces in the current state of awareness of the masses [presumably those who believe "I yam what I yam"], nor brings to them some alien truth from 'above,' as in the banal caricature of Leninism [presumably Brother Jack's of the Brotherhood] widespread today even on the political left."[1] As a "link or pivot between philosophy and the people," the organic intellectual abjures the disinterested posture of the traditional intellectual. Equally important, though, the organic intellectual also combats "much that is negative in the empirical consciousness of the people, to which Gramsci gives the title of 'common sense' . . . [i.e., that] ambiguous, contradictory zone of experience which is on the whole politically backward."[2]

But the zone of common sense is no more contradictory than the zone occupied by these pivotal performers. Both the invisible man as a character and *Invisible Man* as a novel throw into relief the dilemma of such pivotal or connective agents—the putative link between philosophy and the people—for whom the figure of the traitor stands as an uncanny double. On the one hand, because the Brotherhood's decision making takes place at a distance from Harlem and because the protagonist has been away from Harlem for some time, the protagonist and the Brotherhood arouse the suspicions of the Harlemites when their activities seem to cut against the grain of local needs and events. The invisible man warns the committee that the people "accuse us of betraying them" (472). On the other hand, when he is unable to contact the committee and acts on his "personal responsibility" to deliver what the people want, he finds himself suspected of betraying the Brotherhood.

Having assembled a crowd on the strength of their outrage—the crowd knows that Clifton was killed "mainly because he was black"—the narrator poses to the committee the question of whether or not such an assemblage can be further mobilized for leftist political activism. The fact that in the novel the Brotherhood has condescendingly "decided against such demonstrations" (472) does not blunt the force of the narrator's warning about the consequences of not capitalizing on this event ("If we don't follow through on what was done today, this might be the last . . ." [471]). And in many respects, the crucial question raised by this warning still begs an answer. That is, while it is relatively clear how a protest against racial injustice such as police violence or illegal evictions can be readily woven into a web of opposition to social and economic injustice, is it equally clear that a movement centrally turning on racial self-affirmation and expression can lend itself to similar linkages? This question brings into play not only Clifton's funeral but the Million Man March as well, putting under interrogation some of the progressive claims made at the time that leftist involvement in such events as the march, despite the problematic features of the man standing at its center, was warranted because of the event's potential to connect a constituency-poor black Left with a mass black mobilization. How to assess such a claim?

When I first composed this argument as a lecture in the six months following the march, I observed that Louis Farrakhan's glad-handing with Sani Abacha of Nigeria and Ben Chavis's cozying up with black businessmen and entrepreneurs provided strong indication of the political meaning of the Million Man March. I added at the time, however, that matters of political efficacy cannot always be judged in the short run. Since that time, however, nothing much has occurred that calls for a more sanguine view of the event. Even one of the march's erstwhile supporters has had to question what it meant when the "dollars willingly shelled out by black fathers and sons on the Mall [went to] financing man sojourns of Mr. Farrakhan into repressive lands."[3] So that contrary to assertions on the Left about transforming a sow's ear into a silk purse, the history of the march seems to reveal nothing so much as the difficulty of moving from the self-affirmation of identity into an organizationally strong, progressive political movement.

What is it, then, about racial self-affirmation or self-expression that makes it difficult for it to become anything other than self-affirmation? What are its structures? What are its contents? What does it mean to express and affirm oneself, specifically one's racial self?

In Ellison's novel, although the murder of Tod Clifton remains prominent during the funeral, the march and gathering are not so much against something as they are for something. No petitions against police brutality are circulated. No demands are made for the resignation of city officials. Instead, by having his protagonist wonder whether or not politics could "ever be an expression of love," Ellison places the emphasis on what emotion binds the people together rather than on what they intend to do once they have come together. Benedict Anderson's *Imagined Communities* gives us some idea of the structure of these emotions when he observes "that nations inspire love, and often profoundly self-sacrificing love."[4] Politics, according to Anderson, can be a form of love when it manifests as, or mimics the forms of, nationalism. The invisible man seems to know this intuitively. His speech, in which he likens Tod Clifton to an "unknown soldier" (452), could have come from the second chapter of *Imagined Communities*, where Anderson observes that "no more arresting emblems of the modern culture of nationalism exist than cenotaphs and tombs of Unknown Soldiers."[5] And the fact that Clifton, though "known" (the newspapers cover his death), is pushed toward the state of anonymity, and from there out of history, on to the realm of the immemorial—"Tod Clifton's one with the ages" (458)—merely attests to the ineluctable pull of nationalism on the narrator's consciousness. The narrator is able to make Clifton a symbol precisely by divesting him of the specific attributes of his individual biography—the fact that he was selling racist dolls is deemed to be irrelevant. The narrator's symbolic "reading" of Clinton's death certificate drives home his fungibility with other racial "citizens":

> Didn't they scribble his name on a standardized pad? His Race: colored! Religion: unknown, probably born Baptist. Place of birth: U.S. Some Southern town. Next of kin: unknown. Address: unknown. Occupation: unemployed. (458)

The official standardization of the unique individual on the police record is, of course, dehumanizing here, but it is also in a strange way comforting, for it makes Clifton at that moment, like everyone else standing there, not lost, but somehow found and remembered even when the details of the individual life fall out of focus. Of course, the action that galvanizes the assembled masses at the funeral is the singing of a spiritual, led by an old man with "a worn, old, yellow face," whose voice is joined by "the singing mass. It was as though the song had been there all the time and he knew it and aroused it; and I had known it too and had failed to release it out of a vague, nameless shame or fear." The narrator continues:

> But he had known and aroused it. Even white brothers and sisters were joining in. I looked into that face, trying to plumb its secret, but it told me nothing. I looked at the coffin and the marchers, listening to them, and yet realizing I was listening to something within myself, and for a second I heard the shattering stroke of my heart. Something deep had shaken the crowd, and the old man and the man with the horn had done it. (453)

It seems almost sacrilegious to suggest that the unspoken something here is the nation in all its fictive primordialness, but the participation of white brothers and sisters at the outset indicates that race in itself cannot name the emotion here. So perhaps it is the nation invoked by the singing of anthems that is being evoked. As Anderson writes:

> No matter how banal the words and mediocre the tunes, there is in this singing an experience of simultaneity. At precisely such moments, people wholly unknown to each other utter the same verses to the same melody. The image: unisonance. . . . How selfless this unisonance feels! If we are aware that others are singing these songs precisely when and as we are, we have no idea who they may be, or even where, out of earshot, they are singing. Nothing connects us all but imagined sound.[6]

This feeling as described by Ellison and Anderson is indeed selfless, but perhaps only in the way that the infant in the Lacanian mirror stage can be said to be selfless as it finds itself everywhere. The song, or at least its sound, is not new, either for the invisible man or for the gathered throng, because it is something that each of them already knows. Seeing others singing is to see oneself singing, indeed to see oneself as always already singing.

The shared genius of the accounts given by Anderson and Ellison is their discernment of the affinity between song and numbers. For both, bureaucratic enumeration does not stand in contrast to impassioned singing, with the song compensating for the cold anonymity of numbers on a form. Instead, song and numbers subtly reinforce each other. While at the beginning of the century W. E. B. Du Bois had opposed numbers and song in *Souls of Black Folk* with spirituals of the folk trying to elude the statistics of the sociologist, the alchemy of nation resides in its ability to move us precisely with numbers—indeed to spiritualize numbers. Not accidentally, then, at Clifton's funeral the song that sets the multitude to singing is a slave spiritual entitled "Many Thousands Gone," in which every verse, chronicling the hardships and privations of slavery, ends with the refrain "Many thousands gone."

As Anderson points out, the modern nation-state through its periodic census taking and schemes of classification is obsessive about knowing its numbers. In turn, one might say the same about modern races with the qualification that races "know" their numbers—as much as they might distrust them—through the bureaucratic operations of states, and with the further qualification that races are less defined by knowing their exact numbers (for a nation-state, this kind of precision marks its efficiency) than by their knowing that they are numbered in all senses of the phrase. The differences here are important.

Nationalism in its classic form presumes the immortality of the nation. "Nations," Anderson writes, "have no clearly identifiable births, and their deaths, if they ever happen, are never natural."[7] So that while the year 1776 may mark the independence of the thirteen colonies, the story of the American nation as evidenced by the "culture wars" of the 1980s and 1990s is as old as Western civilization itself. By contrast, modern racial thinking, with the specter of Darwinian extinction hovering in the background, is haunted by the possibility that races are not forever—they can die out and disappear, their annihilation being a diabolical blend of "natural" laws and state actions.

That is, while races may claim to trace their roots to the dawn of time, their future in the modern era has been rendered uncertain. Consider, for example, the logic expressed in Toni Morrison's *Song of Solomon* by the character Guitar, as he describes the workings of the racial assassination squad called the "Seven Days":

The only thing left to do is balance it; keep things on an even keel. Any man, any woman, or any child is good for five to seven generations of heirs before they're bred out. So every death is the death of five to seven generations. You can't stop them from killing us, from trying to get rid of us. And each time they succeed, they get rid of five to seven generations. I help keep the numbers the same.[8]

The contrast here between nation and race could not be more striking. The individual's death as a member of a nation confirms the nation's immortality, while the individual's death as a member of a race brings into view the race's mortality. In the former, one dies as one of the innumerable sons or daughters of the fatherland, the individual death bringing glory to one's progenitors; in the latter, one dies as the potential progenitor of subsequent generations, with the individual death foreclosing the possibility of greater numbers.

The degree to which this contrast does not immediately strike us as a stark one may be the result of crucial changes beginning in the second half of the nineteenth century that began to work in the imagining of the nation. The technological efficiency of modern warfare began to make the disappearance of entire nations a thinkable possibility. Abraham Lincoln, confronted with the astonishing number of dead at Gettysburg, concluded his famous speech with the wish that this nation not "perish from the earth." The proliferation of tombs for the Unknown Soldier, Hannah Arendt notes, occurred in the wake of the immense human carnage of the First World War.[9] In fact, Arendt's *The Human Condition* tracks the disappearance during the modern age of the belief that one's actions in the public realm, rather than one's procreative capacities in the private realm, provided the primary guarantee of one's earthly immortality. Arendt writes, "There is perhaps no clearer testimony to the loss of the public realm in the modern age than the almost complete loss of authentic concern with immortality."[10] No longer able to convince its citizens that their actions in the public realm will guarantee their immortality, the nation-state, itself haunted by its own possible annihilation, secures consent from its citizenry in the only way it can imagine, that is, by assuring them of its commitment to them as progenitors, as families. This change was revealed dramatically in the final years of the twentieth century. Anderson's *Imagined Communities* identifies the "modern culture of nationalism" with the phenomenon of these tombs and the requirement that their occupants be unknown. Anderson urges us "to imagine the general reaction to the busybody who 'discovered' the Unknown Soldier's name. . . . Sacrilege of a strange, contemporary kind!"[11] That Anderson overestimated the reaction to such a contingency was demonstrated dramatically in June 1998 when, through the use of DNA testing, the occupant of the Vietnam War Tomb of the Unknowns was identified as First Lieutenant Michael J. Blassie.[12] The event itself was newsworthy, but there was no general cry of outrage. The Veterans of Foreign Wars urged the Pentagon " 'to make every effort' to inter another set of unidentified remains" as an effort to ensure that the Vietnam War was honored in keeping with other twentieth-century wars. Even so, the claim of the Blassie family on the remains was readily seen as superseding the symbolic needs of the nation, and national imagining was not perceptibly affected. According to the *New York Times*, "Ann Mills Griffiths, the executive director of the National League of Families, said the end of the tradition of interring unknown remains should be celebrated."[13] The technology of DNA testing only made manifest what had been an evolving truth of the mid-twentieth century, which was that nations, by and large, had begun to act like races. The logic of the Seven Days in *Song of Solomon* is, on a much smaller scale, the logic of the Cold War—both are a matter of "keep[ing] the ratio the same."[14] Doomsday was a genocidal fantasy simultaneously nurtured and kept at bay by a surreptitious tending to the numbers.

To return, then, to the context of *Invisible Man*, if the black men and women thronged together at Clifton's funeral found themselves moved by the spiritual's reminder that they were numbered, with many thousands gone, the whites in attendance could be similarly moved because in this moment of the ascendancy of race, we all "know" that we are numbered.

To be sure, speaking of race as "ascendant" is not to argue that all "racial" groups wield significant political or economic power. Many such groups, in fact, may be relatively powerless. Nonetheless, because the "raced" individual never appears in public as an individual but always as a portent of her aggrieved numbers, these groups are perceived as powerful or potentially so. Their power is further enhanced by virtue of the fact that these individuals appear not only as raced and numbered, but as members of families.

It should now be apparent why the Million Man March evinced the preoccupations that it did, predicting how many would show up, trumpeting how many did show up, and berating the National Park Service's alleged underestimation of the real numbers. The mobilizing of men in their capacities as members of families echoed Guitar's concerns for the potential loss of generations. And when, at the end of the day, Louis Farrakhan's apparently rambling address veered into the esoterica of numerology ("Consider the number nine"), he might have been consciously or unconsciously flaunting the logic of his mobilization—he was going to tell us all what the day's numbers had meant.

To be sure, many of the participants in the Million Man March asserted the irrelevance of Farrakhan's speech to the day's events.[15] Noting the inattentiveness of much of the crowd to Farrakhan's address, critics and participants have argued that Farrakhan's keynote failed to set the tone for the assembly. In this version of the day, Farrakhan did not, in the two hours he held the stage, express the meaning of the event. He expressed *his* meaning. To the degree that this reading of the march is true, it is true only in a way that inadvertently speaks to the character of the day. The paradox of this apparently public event was that it was not public at all—it had no public voice. Each individual could wander the Mall or sit among friends secure in the knowledge that his private motives for attending were not only as good as, but indeed superior to, the motives of the event's organizers, and need not at all be affected by the differing beliefs and opinions of others in attendance. On this ground, there could be no adjudication between what the "man in the street" thought and what those "on high" thought. Indeed, no such adjudication was called for since any such differences had already been deemed irrelevant. It is no accident, then, that many of the events scheduled as sequels to or imitations of Farrakhan's march have all insisted on the numerical adjective and most have implicitly or explicitly invoked the family: the Million Woman March, the Million Youth March, the Million Family March, the Million Mom March, and so on. And when Spike Lee got around to depicting Farrakhan's march in his film *Get on the Bus*, he placed his characters on a bus from the fictional "Spotted Owl" line to remind us, if we had forgotten, that black males are an endangered species. Nor did Lee's film actually have to get his pilgrims to the Washington Mall for them to feel the effect of the event, which depended on the media exposure it was expected to generate. Being together regardless of one's politics and one's location was what the experience was all about.

For the political Left, the march's essential privateness and its insistence on unity based on the responsibility devolving from our private roles should have been evidence enough of the recalcitrance of Farrakhan's march to progressive transformation. Terry Eagleton's characterization of a leftist political project suggests why this so. In his words, the "more fundamental political question is that of demanding an equal right with others to discover what one might become, not of assuming some already fully-fashioned identity which is merely repressed. All 'oppositional' identities are in part the function of oppression; and in this sense what one might become cannot be simply read off from what one is now."[16] The transformation of, rather than the affirmation of, social identities would be the expected outcome to any progressive project. Within the family, however, one is born automatically as son or daughter with all of the responsibilities and expectations of those roles already imposed before one has fully come into consciousness—except, of course, if one had been born a slave first. What gave Farrakhan's march its urgency was the heightened attention during the 1980s and 1990s to the history of slavery (witness the acclaim accorded to Morrison's *Beloved*) and the way that the slave regime had prevented black men and women from functioning as fathers, mothers, sons, and daughters. During this same period, Hortense Spillers's signal essay, "Mama's Baby, Papa's Maybe," which centers its analysis on the horrors within the hold of the slave ships, wrestles with the conundrum of how to insist on the importance of enabling black fathers to perform their roles without simply reiterating Daniel Patrick Moynihan's 1965 findings that the most pressing social policy for the Negro was to create and support male-headed households.[17]

But what Spillers wrestled with, the Million Man March deemed to be irrelevant in its conviction that for black people merely being a family was a radical act. And as the logic of the march unfolded against the backdrop of what was termed a genocidal and carceral war against black men, merely being black, male, alive, and not behind bars was presumed to be an act of resistance. The only demand was a show of numbers. Whatever intervention black activists on the Left might have hoped to make, their presence could do little but attest to the irrelevance of their politics: for around the reflecting pool at the Washington Mall, what was most important was the arresting image of a finite but unknown number of black men affirming themselves in the privacy of their international visibility. No public words were adequate to what had brought them together because linking them was neither belief nor politics but who they were, or rather who they could be at that moment, which was not quite a million men . . . standing.

Of Southern Strategies

The publication of Howard Zinn's *The Southern Mystique* in 1964 provided the occasion for Ellison's "If the Twain Shall Meet," in which Ellison observes that while "the South has been the center of our national dilemma, both political and moral . . . most intellectuals have never seriously confronted the South or its people."[1] Unable to discern the nuances of white and black southern character, northern intellectuals viewed the south as a monolith of backwardness and embarrassment. Ellison had already made this point in "The Myth of the Flawed White Southerner," which preceded (even though it had been composed after) "If the Twain Shall Meet" in *Going to the Territory*, by contrasting his and Robert Lowell's reactions to President Lyndon Johnson's invitation to attend the 1965 Festival of the Arts at the White House. Lowell had called on his fellow writers to boycott the event in protest of the Vietnam War. Ellison, however, chose to attend, citing the "personal and group history which had shaped my background and guided my consciousness, a history and background that marked a basic divergence between my own experience and that of the dissenting intellectuals."[2] Unfamiliar with the south by way of background and experience, northerners seemed unwilling even to recognize the need to find out whether or not what they had been told about the south had any basis in reality.

Zinn appeared to be an exception. A leftist white historian from the north (his *People's History of the United States* is now something of a landmark), Zinn had spent seven years teaching at Atlanta's Spelman

College and had drawn on that experience to produce a relatively op-
timistic book about the possibility of moving dramatically and quickly
toward racial equality in the south. Zinn argued that southern political
intransigence had been sustained largely by the presumption of southern distinctiveness. Regional and national political progress had been
hampered by the belief that there "was something about Atlanta, about
Georgia, the Carolinas, that marked them off, as with a giant cleaver,
from the rest of the nation . . . something more that went back to cotton
and slavery, stretching into history as far as anyone could remember—
an invisible mist over the entire Deep South, distorting justice, blurring
perspective, and, most of all, indissoluble by reason."[3] *The Southern
Mystique* sought to dispel these beliefs by demonstrating that the south,
both black and white, was more like the north than had been acknowledged and that in this similarity lay the hope for political and social
transformation. Zinn sought to demonstrate that "the specialness of
the Southern mystique vanishes when one sees that whites and Negroes
behave only like human beings, that the South is but a distorted image
of the North, and that we are powerful enough today, and free enough,
to retain only as much of the past as we want. We are all magicians. We
created the mystery of the South, and we can dissolve it."[4]

This optimism both impressed and dismayed Ellison, who praised
Zinn's "effort to see freshly and act constructively," but chided him for
"underplay[ing] the influence of the past" and overlooking "the more
intriguing mystery of culture," which in Ellison's view made up the heart
of the story of the Negro in the south. Zinn may have been an exception among those northern intellectuals who had not recognized the
centrality of the south and the Negro to American national identity, but
he was also the exception that proved the rule: he had seen Negroes in
the south at close range, but "in shrugging off the encumbrances of the
past, he failed to observe them (or even to identify with them) in sufficient depth," thus missing the significance and substance of what he'd
seen.[5] In critiquing Zinn, Ellison touched on a strain of liberal thinking
about the south that extends back at least to the end of the nineteenth
century, when George Washington Cable urged southerners to shed the
vestiges of regional difference that slavery and segregation had created.
A southerner himself, and an admittedly late but ultimately stalwart
convert to the principles of Reconstruction, Cable believed that "the
day must come when the Negro must share and enjoy in common with

the white race the whole scale of *public* rights and advantages provided under American government."[6] And while his essay "The Silent South" (1885) attempts to reconcile southern identity with his pro–civil rights stance, he also expresses along the way little patience for a belief in the ongoing mystification of southern identity. Addressing the 1882 graduating class at the University of Mississippi, Cable coupled his expectation of racial equality with the forecast that as far as the "South" was concerned, "the day must come when that word shall have receded to its original meaning of mere direction and location." There would not be a "New South," rising out of the ashes of the Civil War and redemption, but rather a "No South" erected on the principles of Reconstruction. Cable continued: "I trust the time is not far away when anyone who rises before and addresses you as 'Southrons' shall be stared at as the veriest Rip Van Winkle that the times can show. When you shall say, 'Southerners? South? New South? Sir, your words are not for us.' "[7] If the work of Reconstruction was to be successful, black subordination and southern identity would both disappear. By Cable's logic, the continued production of "Southernness" would signal the persistence of the nation's black population in the status of second-class citizens.

Cable's argument extended to literary culture as well. In his view, the day was at hand when properly enlightened Mississippians would declare, "We shall no more be Southerners than we shall be Northerners. The accidents of latitude shall be nothing to us. We shall be the proud disciples of every American alike who adds to the treasures of truth in American liturature [*sic*], and prouder still if his words reach the whole human heart and his lines of light run through the varied languages of the world." Creative writer and critic would expel any discernible tincture of southernness from their literary work with the thoroughness with which "the Hebrew housewife purged her dwelling of leaven on the eve of the Passover." Only a repudiation of southernness could enable the south to rejoin what Cable termed "the world's thought."[8]

Thus, while Cable predicted the rise of world-renowned writers from the states of the former Confederacy, he did not allow for any such thing as a southern writer or southern literature. The twentieth century as envisioned by Cable would not have produced a body of literature such that, to quote C. Vann Woodward, "no literate Southerner" reading it "could remain unaware of his heritage or doubt its enduring value."[9] Nor in Cable's twentieth century would an activist intellectual like Zinn have been called on to dispel the myth of "the mysterious and terrible South, the Deep South, soaked in the blood of history, of which William Faulkner wrote." The literature written by Mississippians, Georgians, or South Carolinians would have long since lost its regional flavor.

From the point of view of Cable and Zinn, the rise of the twentieth-century southern writer as a *southerner* was a step backward rather than forward. A vibrant southern literature necessarily subtended a politics and culture devoted more to the past than the future. In Zinn's words, "Our overly heavy sense of history has left us unprepared for the possibilities of swift change in the white South. We are too much impressed with the power of the past."[10] The south needed to face the future.

Ellison's critique of Zinn's *The Southern Mystique*, however, took a different view. Ellison argued that the road to an egalitarian future required a confrontation with the past—a past that when looked at properly was an amalgam of southern, Negro, and American identities. So that if for writers like Cable and Zinn a nation that maintained southern and Negro distinctiveness could not guarantee liberty, justice, and equality for all, Ellison and Woodward saw the potential disappearance of these identities as evidence of a national evasion of the truths of the American past and the realities of American culture. Embedded within this disagreement was a larger dispute about whether transforming American society was first and foremost a political or a cultural project.

Ellison's complaint was that Zinn and people like him had mistaken one realm for the other: "It is interesting how often, for an activist, *culture* means *politics!*"[11] And in making this mistake, political activists, Ellison charged, were too ready to accept as true simplistic and formulaic conceptions of the Negro. The political task of the black writer during the 1940s, 1950s, and 1960s was to escape the straitjacket of ideology and to end the nation's effort to evade the fact of Negro humanity.

As revealed by his depiction of the Marxist Left in *Invisible Man*, Ellison had, by the late 1940s and early 1950s, solidified his belief that much politically leftist theorizing about the Negro was hopelessly simplistic and abstract. The "unrecorded history" of the juke joints, beauty parlors, and churches with which the invisible man rebuked Brother Jack following Tod Clifton's funeral was meant to call attention to the deplorably incomplete representations of black life that presumably guided leftist radicals. Ellison believed the novel could serve political ends by being true to the complexity of the human experience. Lawrence Jackson has argued that Ellison's essays in the *New Masses* during the early 1940s took their "cue from Lenin's idea about the role of the vanguard and Stephen Daedalus's notion of metaphysical harmony." Ellison, according to Jackson, "envisioned a revolutionary intellectual movement in which the avant-garde would surpass and then displace the hegemonic bourgeoisie."[12] Art and literature were to be crucial components of this movement. And though by the early 1960s, during the heat of his exchange with Irving Howe, Ellison seemed to be backing off the notion of artists constituting a political avant-garde ("Negroes want no more fairly articulate would-be Negro leaders cluttering up the airways"), he still held to the belief that the writing and critiquing of novels constituted "a small though necessary action in the Negro struggle for freedom."[13] Essay after essay in *Shadow and Act* and *Going to the Territory* elaborate this position, with Ellison arguing that novelists shrugged their responsibility when they failed to take seriously the demands of their craft and instead accepted the truth of self-proclaimed scientific studies of Negro life in painting their pictures of reality. Novels were perhaps most political when their authors remembered to keep in mind that their job was to write fiction that conveyed the truth of life as experienced and not to turn out sociological or political tracts.

Although Ellison's preference for the experiential over the politically didactic in literature aligned him aesthetically with politically conservative intellectuals, Barbara Foley's study of the aesthetics of this period suggests that Ellison's views were broadly shared not only among the anti-Stalinist Left in the 1950s, but also, and perhaps somewhat surprisingly, among U.S. literary Marxists, who in the 1930s tended to describe "proletarian literature's sins against itself" in much the same terms that would be used by the New Critics and New York intellectuals to denounce Marxist aesthetics generally: " 'hysterical revolutionism,' 'lumpy ideology,' 'schematicism,' 'abstraction,' 'abstract ideology,' 'wish-fulfillment,' 'sloganeering.' "[14] As a critic and a writer, Ellison articulated what was a common, although by no means universal, understanding of novelistic practice in which aesthetic concerns enjoyed varying degrees of autonomy from directly propagandistic and didactic requirements. His outlook echoed, rather than contravened, such documents as Richard Wright's "Blueprint for Negro Writing," which cautions that if "writing is demanded to perform the social office of other professions, then the autonomy of craft is lost and writing detrimentally fused with other interests. . . . If the sensory vehicle of imaginative writing is required to carry too great a load of didactic material, the artistic sense is submerged."[15] Whatever their differences, Ellison and Wright were among those left-leaning critics who, like their opponents on the Right, often valued aesthetic success over political clarity.

But while Ellison sought to keep aesthetic sophistication in line with political efficacy, his critical writing, in practice, tended to highlight the inadequacies of politics and social science when it came to understanding human behavior. In his skirmishes with liberals and with social democrats like Irving Howe, he continually reiterated his belief that sociologically and ideologically derived portraits of black life simply could not capture the full humanity of African Americans. As Robert O'Meally writes, "Ellison's encounter at Tuskegee with [Robert Park's] *Introduction to the Science of Sociology* created an accelerated sense of urgency to learn about black American culture and to convert his knowledge into artistic forms."[16] Whether it was in his censures of Robert Park and Edward Burgess, or in the arguments that he leveled against Gunnar Myrdal's *An American Dilemma*, Howe's "Black Boys and Native Sons," and Zinn's *The Southern Mystique*, Ellison maintained that well-meaning white activists/intellectuals unwittingly operated within an ideology that refused to grant black Americans any degree of agency in constructing themselves and the world in which they lived. It was this refusal that prompted Ellison to ask indignantly in his review of *An American Dilemma*, "Can a people . . . live and develop for over three hundred years simply by *reacting*? Are American Negroes simply the creation of white men, or have they at least helped to create themselves out of what they found around them?"[17]

Not surprisingly, then, what contributed most to Ellison's skeptical assessment of the *Southern Mystique* was Zinn's rather uncritical acceptance of Stanley M. Elkins's formulations about black personality in his infamous study, *Slavery* (1959), a book that Zinn credited with "helping me find a direction for my own thoughts."[18] Elkins's controversial study had extrapolated from psychological studies of inmates from Nazi concentration camps to posit the reality of the "Sambo" stereotype, that is, the Negro as "the perpetual child" in the southern United States.[19] This demeaning stereotype of southern blacks was true in Elkins's estimation, not because of innate racial inferiority, but because the repressive conditions that Elkins saw as definitive of U.S. plantation slavery—its existence as a closed system and its interdiction of all interpersonal relationships other than that between master and slave—had created the personality of Sambo. Elkins's intended, progressive argument was that if Sambo had been made, he could also be unmade.

Zinn had seized on the historical contingency of the Sambo personality as reason for political optimism because "the beaten-down and submissive Negro becomes explainable as the product of the plantation's closed society. That personality also becomes, Elkin suggests, 'reversible.' "[20] Here, for Zinn, was further evidence that the south and its people could be changed. For Ellison, however, Elkins's book was occasion for disgust. He chastised Elkins's "Sambo" as the reintroduction of "nineteenth-century white Southern pseudosociology" into "what passes for intellectual discussion."[21] The problem was not only that claims about the plasticity of human personality got their momentum by crediting white Americans' most debasing assumptions about black Americans, but that, by crediting these assumptions, white Americans failed to see their own prejudices and pathologies.

Elkins and Zinn were but two examples. Much of Ellison's intellectual and creative career before the publication of Elkins's book had constituted a repudiation of simplistic accounts of Negro personality.[22] Ellison repeatedly exposed racist stereotypes as whites' projections onto blacks of their own fears and anxieties about being Americans, and he also argued that blacks had often responded to these stereotypes with self-conscious masking and with a manipulation of roles. As he writes in "Change the Joke and Slip the Yoke," the

> Negro's masking is motivated not so much by fear as by a profound rejection of the image created to usurp his identity. Sometimes it is for the sheer joy of the joke; sometimes to challenge those who presume, across the psychological distance created by race manners, to know his identity.[23]

Seeing the Negro correctly required seeing behind his mask and looking beneath the surface of the interactions taking place between blacks and whites on the streets and in the kitchens of southern towns. Northern observers, however, often mistook outward appearance for inner truth and failed in their observations to consider motivation and imagination.

As Ellison jousted with critics and considered the literary productions of his predecessors and contemporaries, the standard of judgment he used was the writer's capacity to acknowledge and then probe beneath the surface of southern social relations. In the realm of novelistic endeavor, Faulkner's ability to "start with the stereotype, accept it as true, and then seek out the human truth which it hides" was one example of how the novelist could rebuke the simplistic formulas of the activist and the social scientist.[24] Yet Ellison had to fight the war on behalf of Negro humanity on two separate if overlapping fronts. If, on the one hand, the political and sociological simplifications of black humanity had to be debunked, it also remained important to discredit the claim that the cultural basis of southern racial inequality made that social system impervious to political and rational solution.

Ellison could not, then, take up a position entirely opposite to Zinn's, although he could insist pointedly that there was more to the matter than Zinn had understood. Ellison writes:

> The Southern Negroes who have *revealed* themselves since 1954 are not products of some act of legal magic; they are the products of a culture, a culture of the Southern states, and of a tradition that ironically they share with white Southerners. But with Negroes it developed out of slavery and through their experiences since the Civil War and the first Reconstruction. . . . [T]he Negro American is something more. He is the product of the synthesis of his blood mixture, his social experience, and what he has made of his predicament, i.e., his *culture*. His quality of wonder and his heroism alike spring no less from his brutalization than from that culture.[25]

Ellison was seeking a dynamic, even dialectical, account of the Negro that would acknowledge the history of racial repression but not characterize black people as merely prisoners of a repressive environment. The challenge he faced was making his account truly dialectical. Too much stress on the autonomy of cultural practices might too readily accommodate southerners who resisted political change by invoking the folkways mentioned by William Graham Sumner.[26] By the same token, an overly historical account of culture might appear to support the claim that the Negro was no more than the sum total of the racist and dehumanizing practices employed against him—that the racist state-ways of the south had succeeded in transforming the Negro into the kind of being that slavery and Jim Crow needed him to be. At their best, Ellison's essays carefully steer between these two obstacles, and yet Ellison's sympathies often tilt toward arguments stressing the autonomy or semi-autonomy of culture, largely because—as he said to Irving Howe—he feared "the social order" portended by white activists more than he feared the social order of segregationist Mississippi. As bad as the latter had been, it had not succeeded in squelching the development of an idea of culture among black Americans—a culture, Ellison was hasty to point out, not confined to folk traditions but composed from an amalgam of traditions and practices. By contrast, the new social order, despite the freedom it promised, seemed capable of viewing the black American as nothing more than a social problem awaiting an adroit solution. If being black was simply to be in "a state of irremediable agony," the only sensible solution was to relieve the nation of its pain.[27] It was perhaps for this reason that Ellison followed "If the Twain Shall Meet" with an essay criticizing "the recurring fantasy of solving one basic problem of American democracy by 'getting shut' of the blacks through various wishful schemes that would banish them from the nation's bloodstream, from its social structure, and from its conscience and historical consciousness."[28] What made the fantasy absurd was the vast absence that would be American culture without blacks: "Without the presence of blacks [*Huckleberry Finn*] could not have been written. No Huck and Jim, no American novel as we know it. . . . Not only would there have been no Faulkner; there would have been no Stephen Crane, who found certain basic themes of his writing in the Civil War. Thus also there would have been no Hemingway, who took Crane as a source and guide."[29]

Of course, Ellison was not the first to fight the analytical disease of seeing the Negro as strictly a problem by administering a dose of the Negro as the heart of American culture. Du Bois, long before him, had made a similar claim when he reminded white America, "Actively we have woven ourselves with the very warp and woof of this nation," and then asked rhetorically, "Would America have been American without her Negro people?"[30] The lesson was clear: If somehow the Negro were magically to disappear, then the *all* of American culture and the specificity of southern culture would have to disappear as well.

This claim of interdependency, however, also raised the counterpossibility. If America and, more specifically, the "South" were likewise to disappear, then would not the Negro as a discrete identity have to follow suit? Were not the American nation and the American Negro so forged in the same blast furnace that liberation from one required liberation from the other? Among those who answered this question in the affirmative was Malcolm X, who, of course, viewed the loss of the Negro as a political gain. In an argument that treated the Negro as merely a figure of racial subordination, Malcolm told a Cleveland audience in 1964, "You're nothing but Africans. Nothing but Africans."[31] But for Ellison, who saw the drama of modern democracy as a story played out between black and white Americans, to give up on Americanness was to give up on the greatness of the democratic experiment.

Ellison's ongoing commitment to the idea of the Negro's southernness requires further consideration, particularly in light of his readiness on certain occasions to argue that his frontier background was part of what set him off from a Mississippi writer like Richard Wright. In *Invisible Man*, shortly after arriving in New York, the protagonist regards his southern origin as the last thing he hoped would follow him on his journey north. When the counterman at a drugstore diner offers him the breakfast special of "pork chops, grits, one egg, hot biscuits and coffee!" the narrator wonders with dismay, "Could everyone see that I was southern!" (178). Urban sophistication, by definition, appears to be antithetical to southern tastes. And yet in a few moments, the counterman will offer the same breakfast to "a man with a pale blond mustache" (179), suggesting that things are not all that settled. Even so, what becomes necessary to the protagonist's journey of self-discovery is his recognition that his southern habits and inclinations are something other than badges of humiliation. The combination of homesickness and freedom he feels merely allowing himself to eat a yam while walking along the street demonstrates that his struggle for self-definition has lacked simple self-acceptance, the same quality he sees as missing from the lives of so many other Negroes: "What a group of people we were, I thought. Why, you could cause us the greatest humiliation simply by confronting us with something we liked. Not *all* of us, but so many"

(264). And what so many of *us* had never permitted ourselves was not a racial taste but a personal one. As the invisible man is forced to admit, he "had never formed a personal attitude towards so much" (267). Prior to that moment, the day-to-day choices that came with living had been assumed preferences, rather than personal ones: things that he was "not supposed to like," distastes that were "considered a mark of refinement and education" (266).

Experiencing this revelation moves the narrator further toward understanding himself and what he should want—but only so far, because "the freedom to eat yams on the street was far less than I had expected upon coming to the city" (267). And to emphasize this point, the novel then confronts the protagonist, who has now begun to respond personally to the world around him, as a onetime southern Negro, with the heartrending eviction of an elderly southern migrant couple, a scene that begins the narrator's career as an orator. Confronted with the litter of the old couple's possessions tossed into the street, the invisible man and those around him cannot avoid an unwilling encounter with shame, "as though, they, we, were ashamed to witness the eviction, as though we were all unwilling intruders upon some shameful event; . . . for we were witnesses of what we did not wish to see, though curious, fascinated, despite our shame" (270). The narrator is riveted to the spot by the shame of dispossession, which he experiences as his own in part because the couple's possessions are a visual allegory of the history of the Negro from slavery through migration, from "FREE PAPERS" to "a yellowing newspaper portrait of a huge black man with the caption: MARCUS GARVEY DEPORTED" (272). He is moved to identify with the old couple's dispossession, "as though I myself was being dispossessed of some painful yet precious thing which I could not bear to lose; something confounding, like a rotted tooth that one would rather suffer indefinitely than endure the short, violent eruption of pain that would mark its removal" (273). That he sees the Negro past, allegorized by the old couple's scattered possessions, as an abscessed tooth whose necessary removal will bring on enormous pain reveals the protagonist's dilemma.

But the simile is not an exact one. The eviction is and is *not* an extraction, for what has been painfully removed and thrust into the light must not be thrown away but returned properly to its place. After the protagonist's words have moved the crowd, he urges them in words triumphantly ironic, "Take it all, hide that junk! Put it back where it came from. . . . Put it out of sight! Hide it, hide their shame! Hide *our* shame!" (281). Put everything back, but differently, he tells them, not because one feels ashamed of what has been revealed, but because one understands how it feels to have been treated shamefully. At the individual level, the challenge of southernness for the Negro requires moving from denial, through painful acknowledgement, and finally to a reintegration of the shameful within oneself—a process that in the novel provides the occasion for the invisible man and others to act together on behalf of the dispossessed.

And yet southernness, as a political concept, has rarely if ever portended a broader democratization of American life. Whether mobilized by planter minorities to persuade non-slaveholding white smallholders to take up arms against the Union (and against their own given interests) during the Civil War; invoked by Dixiecrats in 1948 in opposition to the Truman administration's begrudging support for fair employment, civil rights, and for legislation outlawing lynching, poll taxes, and discrimination in interstate transportation; or employed by Reagan/Bush/Gingrich Republican Party political operatives as a "southern strategy" to create a political opposition to the remnants of Johnson's Great Society programs, southernness has been brandished in opposition to policies and programs that sought to extend the benefits of full citizenship to poor and nonwhite Americans. Given this legacy, the wisdom of Cable's call for a "No South" seems inescapable, even if it were to seal the fate of the Negro as Ellison knew him.

But the ongoing appeal of the south and the Negro derived less from the democratizing potential embodied in each term than from the fond hope that American society might find in both the cultural and spiritual resources sufficient to offset the demoralization and desacralizing of life under the advance of late capitalism. The Negro remained "southern" because both the Negro and the south signaled humanity's capacity through culture to resist the soulless advance of late-twentieth-century technology. The "tragic" reading of southern history and the tragicomic sensibility of the Negro's blues testified to a culture that had enabled human beings to endure, to use Faulkner's words, the horrible truths of the human condition.

If Ellison's objective was to wring from historians and sociologists an admission that they had not adequately considered the question of culture in regarding the Negro, one measure of his success is to be found in the additions that Elkins made to *Slavery* for the third revised edition in 1976. Not only did Elkins add a new introduction acknowledging that "by the end of 1974 it was apparent that another area—black culture—had come to predominate over all other concerns in the study of American slavery," but in an appended chapter entitled "The Two Arguments on Slavery," he also admits that "Ralph Ellison, judging from what others have published over the past few years, has clearly carried his point on black culture."[32]

That is, in Elkins's view, the "intellect and sensibility" of Ralph Ellison's essays had helped give "the search for black culture the authenticity and legitimacy to which it was entitled, and still is entitled."[33] In what seems at first glance a surprisingly generous and astute review essay that makes up the third section of his new chapter, Elkins concedes "the full validity of Ellison's case, adding, however, a proviso that he 'will be taking some of it back later on.' "[34] We will address Elkins's proviso momentarily, but for now it is important to note that Elkins had clearly been stung by Ellison's censure of those scholars who had overlooked what Eugene Genovese referred to in the subtitle of *Roll, Jordan, Roll* as "the world the slaves made."[35] Surveying Ellison's work from 1944 through the late 1960s, Elkins remarks on the consistency with which Ellison pressed his case on culture, a case that Ellison laid out at a moment when white scholars and activists (including Elkins) believed, understandably, that the best argument against a racist society was one emphasizing the "damage" that it had done to its black victims. That this was an argument in which whites addressed whites and in which blacks served as people's exhibit A was, as Elkins is forced to admit, a significant disadvantage, but it was an argument that simultaneously supported and derived its energy from the Civil Rights movement. The bulk of this writing, Elkins avers, functioned

> as both theoretical and ideological underpinning for the movement, and the writers themselves—historians, psychologists, sociologists, or whatever—were well aware of this. Each had contributed details to the catalogue of abuses that white society had heaped upon American blacks beginning with slavery, and of the damage for which, it was now earnestly felt, restitution must at last be made.[36]

The 1960s and the rise of Black Power and black studies had changed all that so rapidly that, according to Elkins, it had left "white intellectuals in rather a state of shock."[37] Had they been reading Ellison astutely, however, their shock would have been lessened considerably because the case against the white Left and liberal paternalism, which was to give so much energy to the Black Power movement of the 1960s, was not a new case but an inherited one, with Ellison as one of its benefactors.

Yet while Elkins found it difficult to gainsay Ellison's eloquence and intelligence on this matter, his concession, as he had indicated, was much stingier than it appears at first glance. As he reviewed the backlash against the Moynihan Report, Elkins made two crucial observations.[38] The first was that the report's hostile reception inaugurated a period when white scholars found themselves routinely intimidated by "an emergently aggressive black audience."[39] Ellison was partly responsible, not only because he had condemned Moynihan publicly (taking the occasion to deal another blow to the hapless Elkins) but because "to chastened whites" Ellison's "appeal [to black culture] was irresistible." Elkins's second observation, which follows logically from the first, was that although the culture-as-resistance thesis had carried the day against Moynihan's "damage thesis," it had done so less by substantive and reasoned argument than by ideology. White historians might indeed have operated with a blind spot regarding black culture, but, according to Elkins, no one had yet sufficiently proved the case for what he took to be Ellison's most telling claim. That is, it had never been sufficiently proved that the culture produced by African Americans under slavery had been more nurturing than damaging. So that while he concedes the existence of a black or Negro culture, Elkins also writes, "It does not follow that simply in locating culture we have automatically found something ipso facto positive, in and of itself." He continues:

> No theory of culture I know of claims that much, though the point is by no means clear in much of the recent discussion of American black slavery. Culture under conditions such as those of slavery is not acquired without a price; the social and individual experience of any group with so little power, and enduring such insistent assaults (of cruelty, contempt, and not least, uncertainty), is bound to contain more than the normal residue of pathology. Any theory

that is worth anything must allow for this. It must allow, that is, for damage.[40]

Damage, according to Elkins, had not been "disproved" but had gone underground.

Ellison, however, had never made such a blanket claim about culture. To the contrary, he had assumed that living a life that did not merely acquiesce in the conditions in which one found oneself always exacted some "price." And had Elkins looked further, he would have discovered, for example, that even Ellison's often-quoted definition of the blues ("The blues is an impulse to keep the painful details and episodes of a brutal experience alive in one's aching consciousness, to finger its jagged grain, and to transcend it, not by the consolation of philosophy but by squeezing from it a near-tragic, near-comic lyricism") painted a far from rosy picture of life under slavery.[41] In fact, even as Ellison elaborated his understanding of the blues in his 1945 review of Richard Wright's *Black Boy*, he also embraced certain characterizations of black life that were not all that distant from some of the claims later made by Elkins and Moynihan. Accepting the work of "the young Negro critic Edward Bland," Ellison affirms that southern black life was "pre-individual." And then in words eerily anticipating Elkins's analogizing of plantation slavery to Nazi concentration camps, he writes, "This pre-individual state is induced artificially, like the regression to primitive states noted among cultured inmates of Nazi prisons."[42] Throughout his review of Wright's autobiography, damage abounds: there are certain "sentiments, attitudes and insights which, as a group living under certain definite social conditions, Negroes could not humanly possess." And the black family, at least for poorer Negroes, seemed to be just as Moynihan depicted them: "The lower-class Negro family is matriarchal," Ellison observes.[43]

The difference between him, on the one hand, and Elkins and Moynihan, on the other, Ellison might have insisted, was that Ellison's account of the limitations that slavery and the south imposed on the Negro never lost sight of the idea "that human life possesses an innate dignity and mankind an innate sense of nobility; that all men possess the tendency to dream and the compulsion to make their dreams reality; that the need to be ever dissatisfied and the urge ever to seek satisfaction is implicit in the human organism."[44] And yet what brought Ellison closer than he might have wanted to admit to the line that Elkins and Moynihan were to take fifteen to twenty years later were the tactical demands of the argumentative moment. Ellison directed his most significant critique at those who believed "that since Negroes possess the richly human virtues credited to them, then their social position is advantageous and should not be bettered, and, continuing syllogistically, the white individual need feel no guilt over his participation in Negro oppression."[45] The urgency of refuting those who claimed that the south was merely different from the rest of the nation and had not built a social order predicated on oppressing its black citizens dictated Ellison's stress on the very "reactive" element of Negro life that a year previously he had censured Myrdal's study for presuming.

In some sense, then, Elkins was right in observing that the "damage thesis" remained lurking in the tall grass of the cultural argument. Culture could not be pure resistance. It had to be accommodating as well as progressive, debilitating as well as nurturing, blinding as well as revealing. Where Elkins's analysis faltered, however, was in its political reading of the historiographical and sociological debate and its subsequent effects. The most important outcome of this moment was not the muzzling of those white scholars and politicians whose analyses of black life were less than flattering. Although a cadre of white left-leaning or former leftist intellectuals—among whom we might include Elkins, Genovese, Stephan Thernstrom, and David Horowitz—apparently believed that the nation's race problem took a turn for the worse when black people stopped listening to them, they greatly overestimated their contribution to the debate. The most significant outcome of the culture-as-resistance versus culture-as-damage debate was the way that it helped retool what were essentially conservative political analyses for use in black "radical" critiques from the late 1960s until the present. The verbal missiles aimed at Moynihan's criticism of the black family did not blast his arguments from the field. Rather, as Adolph Reed notes, "Nationalists and other petit bourgeois black sexists began incorporating Moynihan's charges concerning the existence of a black matriarchy that crushed male spirit and arrested masculine development."[46] These activists readily accepted the notion that considerable psychic damage had been done collectively to blacks by slavery and its aftermath. They felt, however, that diagnosing and redressing this damage fell more properly to capably trained or properly positioned black activists and intellectuals acting on behalf of those too damaged to know what was best for them. In appropriating the damage thesis, nationalists did not overlook the role of black culture, but instead celebrated it as a once-upon-a-time powerful vaccine against the ravages of racism that could now be just what the doctor ordered for a post-industrial world.

Although Ellison was by no means the chief architect of this change, some inkling of how it came about can be gleaned from his work. In reviewing Richard Wright's *Black Boy*, for example, Ellison acknowledges the

> blasting pressures which in a scant eighty years have sent the Negro people hurtling, without clearly defined trajectory, from slavery to emancipation, from log cabin to city tenement, from the white folks' fields and kitchens to factory assembly lines, and which, between two wars, have shattered the wholeness of its folk consciousness into a thousand writhing pieces.[47]

Perhaps more influenced by Chicago school sociology than he realized, Ellison here adopts what was a commonplace social analysis of twentieth-century black America in which folk societies under slavery were argued to have exhibited a cohesiveness and shared sense of identity not evident in modern industrializing societies.[48] As Daryl Michael Scott correctly observes, "Strictures against psychiatric appeals and social science damage imagery notwithstanding, Ellison was not the antipathologist he is often taken to be."[49] For Ellison, the post-emancipation Negro was a more fragmented, more uncertain, more troubled, if more interesting, being than had been his pre-emancipation counterpart. The image of a "people hurtling, without clearly defined trajectory," is the image of a people in need of direction and leadership.

Folk cohesiveness, which served Ellison primarily as a point of departure (his real interest was in the post-emancipation odyssey of black America), assumed a much larger significance in the cultural historiography that Elkins claimed had risen in the wake of his 1959 study. Lawrence W. Levine's *Black Culture and Black Consciousness* argues for a black culture under slavery that had been able to screen out the demeaning stereotypes that whites, generally, and slave owners in particular, projected onto blacks. According to Levine:

The entire sacred world of the slaves . . . created the necessary space between the slaves and their owners and [was] the means of preventing legal slavery from becoming spiritual slavery. In addition to the world of the masters which slaves inhabited and accommodated to, as they had to, they created and maintained a world apart which they shared with each other and which remained their own domain, free of control of those who ruled the earth.[50]

In a very real way, then, the part of Elkins's argument that won out in this debate is the idea of the slave's world as a relatively "closed system." The crucial difference is that in Elkins's argument the insularity of the system permitted the master's power over his slaves to be absolute, while for Levine the psychological influence of the master had been held at bay by a black sacred culture that had reigned successfully within the social enclosure of the plantation.

Almost necessarily, then, Levine's argument has to posit an attenuation of black cultural strength outside the plantation's closed society. "Freedom," Levine writes, "ultimately weakened the cultural self-containment of the slaves and placed an increasing number of Negroes in a culturally marginal situation." Accordingly, black secular forms like the blues, which emerged after emancipation, were more reflective of "the larger society" of the nation than their sacred antecedents had been. (Even here, however, Levine takes care not to make the blues merely a response to early-twentieth-century racism, and he explicitly takes issue with Frantz Fanon's prediction that the blues would disappear with the demise of racism. Black music, Levine avers, was a testament to the capacity of a people to "carve out independent values and standards." Levine argues further that black distinctiveness as an enduring feature of American society could provide a model for understanding group distinctiveness as a whole: "The black experience may well help us to further re-evaluate the entire image and theory of the melting pot. It may help us to understand the process by which many different groups in the United States have managed to maintain a remarkably independent though only partially separate existence."[51]

Levine's goal was to highlight and account for the continuity of black cultural identity. Yet the trajectory of his argument suggests that black vulnerability to psychological damage increased inversely to the loosening of strictures on black political, social, and economic life. Surrounded by their sacred world, slaves were more likely to be psychically whole than their Jim Crow descendants, who in turn had experienced less marginality than their post-segregation successors. The psychic health of twentieth-century black Americans (and all ethnic Americans) depended less on their success in transforming society as a whole than on their conservation of the "strong centripetal urge which continually drew them back to central aspects of their traditions even as they were surging outward into the larger society." The larger world, although it represented "increased opportunity and mobility," also constituted a threat against which groups sought "to guard their values, maintain their sense of worth, and retain their sanity."[52]

The great achievement of this new narrative of the American past was its having shifted the spotlight of history onto the many thousands gone who had crafted a distinctively black culture. History could now be written from the bottom up rather than from the top down with blacks rather than whites viewed as the agents of historical change. As a bonus, the tradition of historical scholarship that celebrated and defended southern difference would find itself discredited. Yet something else seems to have happened. Instead of suffering banishment to the deep shadows of defunct historiography, the heroic narrative of the white south has found itself harboring in the outer glow of the new narrative of American history, in part, perhaps, because the "bottom up" approach defined the methodology of works like U. B. Phillips's *American Negro Slavery*, which reminds scholars that it "is therefore to the letters, journals and miscellaneous records of private persons dwelling in the regime and by their practices molding it more powerfully than legislatures and courts combined, that the main recourse must be had."[53] Scholars like Levine and Genovese, who sought to pay homage to the way black Americans had managed against overwhelming odds to create and sustain a world apart from the dominant and homogenizing forces of the modern era, also provided reasons for admiring anew the white south. And Genovese in his foreword to the 1966 reprinting of *American Negro Slavery* makes clear his sense of indebtedness to Phillips not merely for his scholarship but for his sensibility. Phillips helped him see that the South, white and black, has given America some of its finer traditions and sensibilities and certainly its best manners. These were once firmly rooted in the plantation way of life and especially in the master-slave relationship. Their preservation does not require the preservation of the injustice and brutality with which they were originally and inseparably linked, but it does require a full understanding and appreciation of those origins.[54]

Thus the older narrative of white southern history could be heroic as well because it, too, had been part of a war of resistance to American homogenization in service of the preservation of something fine. What once had been a suspicion that what was good for southern distinctiveness must be bad for the Negro had been transmuted into the notion that preserving southern distinctiveness and maintaining black distinctiveness were part of the same political struggle. One of the more ironically striking ways that the recovery of the south and the recovery of the Negro have gone hand in hand occurs in Houston Baker's *Turning South Again: Re-Thinking Modernism/Re-Reading Booker T.*, which argues for a return to W. J. Cash's *The Mind of the South* as a way of understanding contemporary America and the task lying before black America at the beginning of the twenty-first century. In Baker's view, Cash's "psycho-cultural" reading of the southern mind as a transhistorical entity remains relevant because it "captures . . . the *mind* of America in providing a comprehensive analysis of what he called the *South*." Baker's call for a recentering of American studies in the south is not an argument for southern culture as an alternative to market society. Rather, Baker's claim that "the United States at large is always already in Mississippi, and Mississippi—for better or worse for black modernism—is always in the United States" is an attempt to make his readers understand that the confinement of the plantation, the work farm of the late nineteenth and early twentieth centuries, and the contemporary prison are all part of the same historical/political landscape. It was in these "tight places" that "the souls of black folk gave way to a brilliant expressivity, canny improvisation, striking innovations, black mobility of body and mind, and arguably, a cosmopolitan and liberatory *cultural* discourse that would have captivated even Baudelaire."[55] The mechanism is different but the result is more or less the same:

black distinctiveness is preserved by rediscovering the southernness of America.

Strictly speaking, the contemporary linking of the south and the Negro could be claimed to mark no shift at all from earlier work. Du Bois in *Souls of Black Folk* had argued that "the faithful, courteous slave of other days, with his incorruptible honesty and dignified humility" was "passing away just as surely as the old type of Southern gentleman is passing, and from not dissimilar causes,—the sudden transformation of a fair far-off ideal of Freedom into the hard reality of bread-winning and the consequent deification of Bread."[56] But as David Greenberg has pointed out, the post-Elkins reemphasis of the psychic, cultural, and spiritual resources of blacks under slavery risked becoming U. B. Phillips "lite" in which the New Left's argument "that slaves were sometimes happy *despite* their condition as slaves . . . inadvertently dovetails with the right's racist interpretations" of slavery as a relatively benign institution.[57] Of course, the objective of these right-wing interpretations has not been to bring back slavery as an institution. Rather, the point is to support the idea that the human condition is so greatly determined by cultural and spiritual factors that institutional and materialist critiques and solutions are always inadequate to explaining and alleviating human misery. Redressing society's ills required that groups take responsibility for the cultural habits that presumably reinforced behaviors detrimental to succeeding in the larger world.

One strange effect of this cultural turn has been the way that across the political spectrum many individuals who expressed concern about the economic and social plight of black urban populations in the 1980s and 1990s began to find it rhetorically compelling to contrast the post-segregation present unfavorably with the Jim Crow and slave pasts.[58] From extreme statements like Dr. Eugene Rivers's complaint that many black young men in the 1980s were growing up unfit even for slavery to William Julius Wilson's ostensibly "more" moderate observations lamenting the demise of what he described as socially organized even if segregated black communities of the 1950s came the view that black people had been emotionally and spiritually happier and healthier (if economically worse off) under slavery and during Jim Crow than at present. The marvelous black culture that had survived virtually intact through some of history's most devastating horrors was suddenly on the brink of internal collapse.[59] As Cornel West puts it, while in the past our "black foremothers and forefathers" had created "powerful buffers to ward off the nihilistic threat, to equip black folk with cultural armor to beat back the demons of hopelessness, meaninglessness, and lovelessness," by the 1980s "the cultural structures that once sustained black life in America [were] no longer able to fend off the nihilistic threat."[60]

West's diagnosis of the state of contemporary black America added to a chorus of cultural and political commentary intoning that if the northern migration of black Americans to urban cities over the course of the twentieth century had been successful, its success was due to the fact that blacks had carried with them to Chicago, New York, and other points north the "cultural armor" forged in the cotton, rice, and cane fields. We may indeed have left the south, but thankfully the south has not left us. Not, that is, for the time being. But as Toni Morrison has argued in her critical essays, interviews, and fiction, the urban world has struck back with a vengeance, and as a result, she writes, "my people are being devoured." There was a need to discover something that could perform the life-sustaining functions that black "music used to do." According to Morrison, "The music kept us alive, but it's not enough anymore." Fiction would be required to fill in the gap: "village literature, fiction that is really for the village, for the tribe." Novels would help the tribe "identify those things in the past that are useful and those things that are not."[61]

So as they surveyed the social scene from Princeton University in the late 1980s and early 1990s, writers like Morrison and West added their voices to the growing consensus that perhaps the most important political project facing black academics and writers in the waning decades of the twentieth century was to preserve and revitalize the village culture that had existed in the past, possibly among African societies but most certainly during the slave era in the U.S. south. West's *The Ethical Dimensions of Marxist Thought*, which seeks to draw from "the best work of Raymond Williams, W. E. B. Du Bois, Eugene Genovese, and Simone de Beauvoir," calls for "a progressive cultural renaissance that reshapes our values, restructures how we live, and puts struggle and sacrifice closer to the center of what we think and do. Only then will our fight to turn back a market-driven, conservative United States—already far down the road to social chaos and self-destruction—be not only desirable but also credible."[62]

Which culture or cultural elements, however, were to be reawakened? Eugene Genovese, for example, was only too ready to assert that dreams like West's—that is, dreams of preserving culture not only as a thing apart from the market but also as a force capable of turning "back a market-driven, conservative United States"—could only be realized through a rehabilitation of southern conservative thought. In Genovese's words, "If we are to recover a sense of national purpose and moral consensus—then southern conservative thought, shorn of its errors and irrationalities [i.e., slavery and racism], has at least as strong a claim to a respectful hearing as any competing body of doctrine."[63] And while West had not explicitly intended to seek a rapprochement with southern conservatism per se, his book *Race Matters* signals his willingness to learn from the people he terms "conservative behavioralists."

In *Race Matters*, West calls for a "politics of conversion" at the center of which is a "love ethic" that constitutes "a last attempt at generating a sense of agency among a downtrodden people."[64] Through this politics of conversion, West sees himself as charting a third way between the limits of "liberal structuralists" and conservative behavioralists. Locating his concept of a "love ethic" "in Toni Morrison's great novel *Beloved*," West declares that Morrison's work "can be construed as bringing together the loving yet critical affirmation of black humanity found in the best of black nationalist movements, the perennial hope against hope for trans-racial coalition in progressive movements, and the painful struggle for self-affirming sanity in a history in which the nihilistic threat *seems* insurmountable."[65] Though he sought to palliate his left-of-center critics by sprinkling his analysis with terms like "progressive movements," "grassroots democratic organizations," "collective leadership," and so on, the view to which West refers, if one actually reads *Beloved*, does not yield forth a democratic vision but rather a religious, therapeutic community. The vision at the heart of Morrison's novel is one in which, for the most part, black politics of the post–Civil War era are scrupulously kept offstage and the crucial scene of social redemption is brought about by the agency of "singing women" whose voices create a "sound that broke the back of words."[66]

As readers of Morrison's novel will recall, Sethe's killing of her daughter leads the local black inhabitants to ostracize her and her family. Based on the story of Margaret Garner, a slave mother who had been driven to the extreme of killing one of her children, *Beloved* constitutes an imaginative argument about the consequences of being isolated from one's broader culture and the pathology resulting from not yet having faced the sometimes horrific truths of one's own history. The novel is as much the story of the surrounding community as it is the story of Sethe's particular trauma. Resentful of the ostentatious feast that Baby Suggs (Sethe's mother-in-law) had put on to celebrate Sethe's freedom, ashamed and guilty for not having warned Sethe of the arrival of the slave catchers, and horrified that a mother could cut the throat of one of her children in an attempt to kill them all to avoid having them returned to slavery, the people of the town leave the family alone and unsupported. Immediately after the killing, as Sethe is being led away, the women fail to sing, they fail to wrap her with "a cape of sound." And when she is released from jail, they refuse to welcome her back into their society. Even years later when the townspeople come out for the funeral of Baby Suggs, who had "devoted her freed life to harmony," the event becomes "a regular dance of pride, fear, condemnation and spite."[67]

Sethe's reincorporation into society occurs only after Ella, who had been formerly a friend to Baby Suggs and Sethe, hearing that Sethe is being killed by the reincarnated ghost of her slain daughter, decides that enough is enough: "Whatever Sethe had done, Ella didn't like the idea of past errors taking possession of the present. Sethe's crime was staggering and her pride outstripped even that; but she could not countenance the possibility of sin moving on in the house, unleashed and sassy." The matter is discussed at the grassroots of the social order, and Ella, a "practical woman who believed that there was a root either to chew or avoid for every ailment," manages to convince "the others that a rescue was in order." And once convinced, "thirty neighborhood women" go out to 124 Bluestone to rescue Sethe with their voices, to provide her the cape of sound they had denied her years ago. They begin to sing and create a "wave of sound wide enough to sound deep water and knock the pods of chestnut trees. It broke over Sethe and she trembled like the baptized in its wash."[68] And this time, redemption is achieved. The women's baptism of Sethe with the sound of their voices effectively exiles Beloved and brings Sethe and Denver back into society.

While this redemptive sequence works powerfully within the novel, it also displays quite chillingly the power a society can exert over the individual. Long after the legal authority has released Sethe from jail, the men and women of her community continue implacable in their judgment of her pridefulness. Against this judgment, Sethe might possibly have asked forgiveness, which she refuses to do, but aside from this, she has no recourse. The will of the community is sovereign. So that when the women finally decide, at the insistence of Ella (who had earlier been equally insistent that Sethe had placed herself outside of social obligation) to rescue Sethe, they do so out of a newfound concern about her plight and not because she as an individual has any power to compel them to act on her behalf. The redemption that Morrison depicts is indeed collective, but more spiritual than political, more intuitive than deliberative, more mystical than logical.

Cornel West is eager to find within *Beloved* the ethos of a democratic order. The social vision at the heart of Morrison's novel, however, is one in which the collective can indeed act redemptively and lovingly toward an individual, but can also choose, without due process, "not to give her the time of day" if she is deemed to have violated its moral beliefs.[69] That is, this vision has less to do with radical democracy than with the kind of southern traditionalism that Eugene Genovese extols in his book *The Southern Tradition*.

Genovese hovers like a half-incarnate ghost over much of West's work. Cited explicitly as an influence in West's *The Ethical Dimensions of Marxist Thought*, Genovese expresses a fear of nihilism and the market in terms almost indistinguishable from West's.[70] Both men also take up the challenge issued by Eugene Rivers's "On the Responsibility of Intellectuals in the Age of Crack," with Genovese echoing many of the other participants in that debate, saying, "One thing seems clear: any effort by the black community to combat social decay and mobilize for an effective political struggle depends upon its ability to rebuild that community."[71]

The force of Genovese's intervention, however, was to make explicit the logic of these observations, a logic that many of the other participants were content to leave incomplete. Rebuilding community through churches and other spiritual organizations would require, according to Genovese,

> imposing considerable social discipline and reining in anti-social
> elements. Mr. Rivers has described a "reconstruction of civil

society in the black community," and suggested that the struggle to restore a stable family life may well lie at the core of that reconstruction [think here of the conclusion of *Beloved*]. More broadly, to speak of "community" at all means to recognize as unavoidable the existence of community prejudices, whether grounded in historically or religiously sanctioned sensibility or in response to an immediate threat to survival. Whites have a responsibility to support the efforts of black communities to solve such problems in their own way and in accordance with their own preferences and prejudices, so long as standards of common decency prevail.[72]

Genovese's willingness to grant rather extraordinary powers to local communities "in their own way and in accordance with their own preferences and prejudices" may help expose the way in which the cultural thesis, which holds that black southern practices and beliefs have protected and nurtured blacks from the psychic ravages of slavery and racism, and the damage thesis, which holds that slavery and Jim Crow blasted black personality, rather than being in conflict have come to complement one another.[73] Those arguing on behalf of the existence of a vibrant black culture had never quite persuaded themselves that Sambo was only a perfervid projection of a white imagination captivated and appalled by the idea that it actually could make up (perhaps indeed *had* made up) blacks from whole cloth. Had the charge rested here (consider, for example, Ellison's rebuke to Howe that Negro life was "no mere abstraction in someone's head"[74]), then writing the history of Sambo would have been writing the history of strategies of racial domination.

Proponents of the cultural arguments, however, had not dismissed Sambo entirely. They rewrote him as a cautionary tale in which blacks under slavery and Jim Crow would have become Sambo but for their considerable success at constructing a unique and rich culture. Wherever there was a distinct and semi-autonomous black culture, then, there, by definition, Sambo—that hapless being able to see himself only as whites in power depicted him, without self-knowledge, without self-consciousness, without self-respect—could not exist. But as we have seen, when these same critics turned their attention to the withering effect of consumer capitalism on black culture, they saw a different picture. To quote Cornel West again:

Many black folk now reside in a jungle ruled by a cutthroat market morality devoid of any faith in deliverance or hope for freedom.

. . . The eclipse of hope and collapse of meaning in much of black America is linked to the structural dynamics of corporate market institutions that affect all Americans. Under these circumstances black existential *angst* derives from the lived experience of ontological wounds and emotional scars inflicted by white supremacist beliefs and images permeating U.S. society and culture.[75]

Sambo and his more sinister cousins had leapt from the white imagination onto the streets of U.S. urban centers, which themselves have been transformed to jungles, where they were now to become the wards of well-intentioned black professionals ready to recivilize them and love them toughly out of their depravity and pathologies. With concerned whites ready to grant to those presumably in charge of the black community the room and autonomy—"so long as standards of common decency prevail"—to get the job done, we find ourselves in a world where the presumed pathologies and behavioral shortcomings of the lower orders are taken to be symptomatic of a failure on the part of natural, organic authorities to impose order upon and exact obedience from the nation's impoverished citizens. From this point of view, the people at the bottom of the social order are—through no fault of their own—just niggahs and will do whatever it is they do unless we—using *almost* any means necessary—decide to stop them.

To Move without Moving:
Reconstructing the Fictions of Sociology

Stanley Elkins was not the only voice crediting Ellison with having crippled white social science. In 1973 Joyce A. Ladner introduced an edited collection of essays, *The Death of White Sociology: Essays on Race and Culture*, with the observation that the "greatest critics of mainstream sociology have been literary men, not sociologists."[1] Accordingly, Ladner added to a volume that featured articles by such black social scientists as E. Franklin Frazier, Ronald W. Walters, James Turner, William E. Cross Jr., and Kenneth B. Clark the "provocative critiques" of Ralph Ellison and Albert Murray. Ellison is represented by his review of Gunnar Myrdal's *An American Dilemma* with its harsh assessment of Robert Park. Murray's contribution, "White Norms, Black Deviation," takes on the Moynihan Report and the misuse of statistics.

Ladner's introduction, like Ellison's and Murray's essays, faults traditional sociology for having failed "to explore the unique experiences and culture of Blacks," a failure that had resulted in a portrait of "Blacks as [a] disorganized, pathological" group defined by " 'cultural deprivation,' 'innate inferiority,' 'social disadvantagement,' and [a] 'tangle of pathology.' "[2] Ladner also agrees with Ellison that Park was largely to blame for creating this impression—an assessment concurred by some of the volume's other contributors. And yet, possibly because Franklin Frazier was Park's student, the volume is not unremitting in its critique of the Chicago sociologist. Indeed, the first essay, jointly authored by John Bracey, August Meier, and Elliott Rudwick, tempers its criticism of Park by noting that "probably no other person could have facilitated the transition of sociology's stance from racism to an attempt at objectivity in racial studies."[3] Even so, the authors follow Ellison in lamenting the inherent racial bias "evident in the early writings of some of American sociology's founding."[4]

Ladner's volume can be seen as another brief in a long-standing case against "white" sociology—a case that predated Ellison and was at least as old as Du Bois's chastisement of white sociologists in the *Souls of Black Folk*, whom he pictured as "gleefully" counting black prostitutes and illegitimate births to black mothers.[5] Nor were Ellison and Murray Du Bois's only allies. Alain Locke before Ellison, and James Baldwin after him, had also weighed in on white sociology's sins. In the mid-1920s, Locke celebrated the northward-bound "New Negro" as a creature undreamt of by sociology.[6] And three decades later, Baldwin insisted that "literature and sociology are not one and the same; it is impossible to discuss them as if they were."[7]

Yet the considerable prestige of sociology's critics had not apparently carried the day against the discipline. The publication of Ladner's volume was evidence that the perception of sociology's predominance in matters concerning black Americans had continued with little diminution through the 1970s—and beyond. If her title was meant to serve as an obituary, the death it announced was premature. Well into the 1980s, Henry Louis Gates Jr. still found it necessary to renew the complaint that sociology's effect on our understanding of black reality remained pernicious. Gates charged that under the misguided influence of sociology,

> black writers themselves seem to have conceived their task to be the creation of an art that reports and directly reflects brute, irreducible, and ineffable "black reality," a reality that in fact was often merely the formulaic fictions spawned by social scientists whose work intended to reveal a black America dehumanized by slavery, segregation, and racial discrimination, in a one-to-one relationship of art to life. Black literacy, then, became far more preoccupied with the literal representation of social content than with literary form, with ethics and thematics rather than poetics and aesthetics. Art, therefore, was argued implicitly and explicitly to be essentially referential. This theory assumed, first of all,

that there existed a common, phenomenal world, which could be reliably described by the methods of empirical historiography or else by those of empirical social science.[8]

As Gates saw the matter at that time, inquiries into black life often failed to realize that while some intellectual tasks, such as representing literally and empirically the often bleak realities of black life, might be sociological, other tasks—namely, the creation of fictions that willingly exposed their fictiveness for the purpose of granting pleasure and enjoyment—were more properly aesthetic or literary. Redressing this mistake became a preoccupation of Gates's early work, which at its base level appears merely to insist that artists and literary critics, on the one hand, and social scientists, on the other, reach an agreement about a sensible division of scholarly labor over things "black."

Gates's words, however, also raised a more serious objection to sociology's influence on literature. Black writers and critics had not only mistaken their aesthetic mission for a sociological one, but, more importantly, they had also failed to recognize that sociology had perpetrated a bait and switch on its literary adherents: under the guise of presenting literally true representations of black life, social science had palmed off tendentious "formulaic" fictions as the truth about black reality. As James Baldwin had put the matter decades before Gates's critique, novels of protest, in their eagerness to represent reality sociologically, instead became "fantasies, connecting nowhere with reality."[9] Sociology's problem was that it frequently missed the very reality it purported to give us.

Gates's critique derived in part from the poststructuralist challenge to the project of representation as a whole: to regard sociology as a more or less objective discipline was a mistake because it was impossible for any putatively objective discipline to represent accurately a world out there. This poststructural critique enabled Gates to reveal how sociology and the fiction that emanated from it were only formulas. Even so, the heart of Gates's complaint was merely an update of Baldwin's attack on Wright. Gates's disparaging observation that the "House of Black Fiction is strewn with dead rats and cockroaches that feed off the ashen-pale bodies of dumb and, of course, wealthy white girls"[10] retreads Baldwin's charge that the sociological vision of Richard Wright had dominated representations of black life.

Wright was certainly an apt target. Called upon to write a preface for St. Clair Drake and Horace R. Cayton's *Black Metropolis*, Wright declared that "huge mountains of fact piled up by the Department of Sociology at the University of Chicago gave me my first concrete vision of the forces that molded the urban negro's body and soul." Wright credited Park, Robert Redfield, and Louis Wirth with giving him the "meanings" that he incorporated into *Twelve Million Black Voices* and his epoch-making novel *Native Son*.[11] Negro reality as Wright had come to know it had been illuminated by sociology.

By centering his objections on the Wrightean turn in black representation, Gates left open the possibility that if sociology could become less a prisoner of its own fictions, it might possibly reflect more accurately the variegated nature of black social life. The main problem, then, was not the project of representation tout court, but the distorted representations that for too long had held sway over the black world. Although Gates's critique of Wright is oversimplified (Cheryl Wall reminds us that Wright was no simpleton when it came to matters of representation and that he cautioned writers against "a too literal translation of experiences into images" and took an approach to aesthetics that was "more nuanced than is sometimes acknowledged"[12]), it is nonetheless useful to consider the extent to which Gates's complaint about sociological dominance rings true.

In an essay published in the *American Review* in 1923, the same year that Jean Toomer's *Cane* appeared, Robert Park exemplified the confidence of the sociologist that black literature was first and foremost an object of sociological study. Discussing Negro poetry, Park wrote, in words that were soon to become infamous:

> My interest in this poetry is not that of a student of literature, but of a student of human nature. I cannot and shall not attempt to speak in the language of literary criticism. But I am disposed to accept quite literally, not as a figure of speech, but as a matter of fact, Mr. Kerlin's statement that a "people that is producing poetry is not perishing, but astir with life, with vital impulses and life-giving visions." It certainly is true, also, more true if possible of the Negro than of any other people, that the Negro poetry is a transcript of Negro life.

> The Negro has always produced poetry of some sort. It has
> not always been good poetry, but it has always been a faithful
> reflection of his inner life. Expression is, perhaps, his metier, his
> vocation.[13]

It was this last sentence, of course, coupled with Park's labeling of the
Negro as "the lady of races," that provoked Ralph Ellison to write in
dismay: "Imagine the effect such teachings have had upon Negro students!"[14] If, however, we tease out some of the assumptions and implications of Park's words, a few curious features emerge. Park does
acknowledge a distinction between a sociological and an aesthetic interest in literature, a distinction that he marks, despite his protestations
to the contrary, by making an aesthetic evaluation: much of this poetry
is not, in his estimation, "good," according to the criteria by which we
generally evaluate literature. Nonetheless, black poetry remains compelling to Park because it is a "transcript of Negro life."

But while Park does, to a large degree, corroborate the charge of a
sociological usurpation of black literature by suggesting that most of
black literature is of interest only because it exists in a one-to-one relationship with black reality, there are a couple of important wrinkles in
his argument vis-à-vis Gates's charge. The first concerns the nature of
what Negro literature is said to be reflective. For Park, the referent of
black poetry is not the brute reality of an impoverished urban existence
that Gates claims had come to dominate literary representation, but
rather the Negro's "inner life." That is, to the degree that Negro poetry
is sociologically interesting for Park, it is so because it reflects not the
group's external conditions but rather its subjective responses to those
conditions. A second point, related to the first, is that if sociology defines
its goal as revealing the inner life of the individuals who make up social
groups, then, at least with respect to the Negro, for whom "expression
is . . . his metier," poetry becomes a proper sociological object. The ob-
viousness of Park's romantic racism does not need further comment
at this point. More important is the way that Gates's critique of sociology repeats rather than refutes some of Park's central assumptions.
Although Park differs from Gates in assuming the transparency of literature in relation to something other than itself, both he and Gates
are alike in placing poetry at the center of black life. Poetry in both

cases tells us who black people are. To Park, poetry enables the Negro to say exactly what he means—expressiveness being almost innate, he cannot help but to reveal just who he is. For Gates, black people are defined by the self-referential use of language that he refers to as "sig-nifyin(g)." According to Gates, "Some historically nameless community of remarkably self-conscious [black] speakers of English defined their ontological status as one of profound difference vis-à-vis the rest of so-ciety."[15] Black literature tells us something about who black people are. If through "signifyin(g)" black people substitute rhetoric for meaning, and through this act of signifyin(g) define their difference from the rest of society, then, somewhat paradoxically, nonreferential language use becomes self-revelatory: black people in Gates's estimation are indeed those people who don't say directly what they mean.

Gates's complaint about sociology assumes a discipline defined by its focus on external social facts such that it was possible to say, "Describe to me a person's external conditions, and I will tell you what thoughts that person might have." Park, on the other hand, describes a sociologi-cal mission that is decidedly more literary than Gates allows for. Recent scholars of the Chicago school have noted the high value it placed on culture. Elizabeth Long writes, "American sociology had a profoundly cultural bent from the start. For example, when American sociology first gained full-fledged disciplinary status as a department at the Univer-sity of Chicago, two of its framing texts devoted considerable attention to culture, establishing forms of sociocultural analysis that became the hallmarks of important traditions within the field."[16] Confessing that it was "from reading Faust" that he derived "the ambition to know human nature, know it widely and intimately," Park writes:

> While I was at Harvard, William James read to us one day his essay on "A Certain Blindness in Human Beings." I was greatly impressed at the time, and, as I have reflected upon it since, the ideas suggested there have assumed a steadily increasing signifi-cance.
>
> The "blindness" of which James spoke is the blindness each of us is likely to have for the meaning of other people's lives. At any rate what sociologists most need to know is what goes on behind the faces of men, what it is that makes life for each of us either dull or thrilling. For "if you lose the joy you lose all." But the thing that

gives zest to life or makes life dull is, however, as James says, "a personal secret" which has, in every single case, to be discovered. Otherwise we do not know the world in which we actually live.[17]

The literary catalyst for Park's sociological ambitions, though, turns out to be less important than his assertion that getting to know others is a supremely difficult intellectual task. And while Park's humanism contrasts with the post-Enlightenment stance that Gates adopted to write *The Signifying Monkey*, Park's view is consistent with Gates's discussion of Frederick Douglass's various biographies in *Figures in Black*. In this text, Gates's rhetorical interests take a decidedly humanist road. Remarking that so few of Douglass's biographers had been able to give us a personal view of their subject, Gates calls for a scholarship that "in full rhetorical power can create a life of Frederick Douglass that somehow gives us a sense of the complexities of the man and of the contradictions among the three public selves he recorded so eloquently in his autobiographies. Perhaps a great scholar can restore to the life of Douglass its decidedly human face."[18] Like Park, Gates's goal was to discover "what goes on behind the faces of men."

Underwriting the resemblance between Gates and Parks is the belief that black cultural practice should preserve some degree of black cultural particularity and specificity. For Park, the Negro's literature becomes less compelling sociologically as it came to resemble modern literature generally. Park concludes:

> Much of the poetry that Negroes write today is like much of our own—interesting but unconvincing. It has form but not conviction. Negro writers, however, have the inspiration of a great theme [nationalism], and occasionally, when their songs arise spontaneously out of a deep racial experience, they speak with an authority of deep conviction and with a tone of prophecy.[19]

I have already noted that Park published his essay the same year Boni & Liveright brought out Jean Toomer's *Cane*. Both texts register the effect of increasing urbanization on the nation's black population, and both, to different degrees, suggest that what is most compelling about black cultural expression was also in danger of fading away. Toomer believed the folk who had sung and lived the spirituals were passing out of existence; correspondingly, after *Cane* he turned explicitly to an amalgamationist cultural and social model.[20] By the same token, Park often discussed black urbanization in terms of a process of interracial adjustment that predicted "racial competition, conflict, accommodation, and eventually assimilation."[21] Yet he also noted with approbation the "disposition of the Negro in America today . . . to accept the racial designation that America has thrust upon him and identify himself with the people whose traditions, status, and ambitions he shares."[22] Consequently, he applauded the Negro for meeting the modern state of restlessness not with a concomitant aimlessness but with a sense of purpose. According to Park, the Negro "is restless, but he knows what he wants. The issues in his case, at least, are clearly defined."[23] What should be kept in view, then, is that for Park an interest in black literature seemed to depend heavily on the capacity of the black population to maintain a sense of itself as a group—a group that remains available for sociological study—even as he formulated a sociology in which groups were all subject to "ineluctable historical and cultural process; the processes by which the integration of peoples and cultures have always and everywhere taken place."[24]

Likewise Gates's *The Signifying Monkey* alludes momentarily to the expectations that in the post-*Brown* world, black particularity would become a phenomenon of a bygone era, only to note with apparent relief that the opposite seems to have been true. The black vernacular was

> thriving despite predictions during the civil rights era that it would soon be a necessary casualty of school desegregation and the larger socioeconomic integration of black people into mainstream American institutions. Because de facto segregation of black and white schoolchildren has replaced de jure segregation, and because black unemployment in 1988 is much higher than it was in 1968, it is impossible for us to determine if black vernacular English would have disappeared under certain ideal social conditions. It has not, however, disappeared.[25]

Gates's recourse to socioeconomic realities should be at least somewhat surprising given his desire to disconnect aesthetics from sociology in considerations of black literature. One might have expected that his insistence on the textual rather than the experiential origin and reproduction of blackness should have enabled him to adopt a posture of indifference toward these social indices. And yet by citing de facto segregation and unemployment statistics, Gates secures his claim for the ongoing vitality of the black vernacular by smuggling into his arguments the very "brute" and "irreducible black reality" that he otherwise disparages in his calls for a properly aesthetic criticism of black literature. So that if at first glance Gates's complaint against sociology appears to be a wish for its disappearance, his trundling in of sociological evidence—perhaps much like Harvard's hiring of the erstwhile University of Chicago sociologist William Julius Wilson, who more or less coined the term the "underclass" even as he argued for the declining significance of race—reveals how much Gates's aesthetic consideration of African American literature depends on what he has termed a sociological formula or fiction.

One constant in Wilson's formula for representing black cultural practice is the putative "social isolation" of poor black city-dwellers. As defined by Wilson and others, social isolation describes the condition created in part by the out-migration of the black middle class from cities to suburbs. In Wilson's view, the "outward mobility for the black working and middle classes removed an important social buffer that could have deflected the full impact of the prolonged and high level of joblessness in these neighborhoods. . . . [O]utmigration of higher-income families and increasing and prolonged joblessness make it considerably more difficult to sustain basic neighborhood institutions."[26] To label "social isolation" a fiction or a formula is not to gainsay the residential, educational, and economic segregation that persists in large cities, nor is it to deny that these patterns of segregation often track with substandard schooling, lower property values, diminished access to goods and services, as well as higher crime rates. Yet we should recognize that there is no set way of defining the boundaries of neighborhoods, nor is there any clear-cut way to decide what counts as being isolated. Albert Murray notes acerbically that "most of the plans and programs for the rehabilitation of places like Harlem and Watts begin with studies that find such places are 'ghettoes' which suffer, as a result of being somehow blocked away from the rest of New York and Los Angeles. Every failing of man and beast is attributed to the inhabitants of such places."[27]

And even when geographical and sociological boundaries are "determinable," they do not always map onto "the boundaries of the social and cultural worlds of the individuals who live within them."[28] People are socially isolated largely because social scientists and policy makers deem them to be so. Of course, in Wilson's estimation, it is the socially isolated black poor who prove most incapable of creating or maintaining the institutions necessary to impose order and social control in their daily lives. These isolated, disorganized people are said to be unable to sustain a culture that would shield them from the shocks and distresses of modern life.

Gates's celebration of a resourceful black vernacular and its various signifying practices thriving in the still-segregated inner city appears to stand at odds with Wilson's bleak picture of a culturally bereft black inner city falling apart at the seams. Yet in his public pronouncements on black America, Gates has been all too ready to posit the idea of an underclass desperately in need of leadership from the talented fifteenth of black America.[29]

This open handshake between Gates and Wilson suggests that the disparaging depictions of impoverished black Americans associated with sociology have persisted not in spite of, but, paradoxically, in part because of "literary men." Gates's certainty that the major task facing black literary scholarship in the 1980s was locating those features that produced black difference and distinctiveness had one logical corollary: the survival of black criticism required the survival of black difference. Scholars were enjoined to account for the historical or—in Gates's case—the textual emergence of group distinctiveness. And this accounting for difference subtly shaded over into the act of reproducing difference, not because scholars intended to reproduce inequality but rather because the reproduction of distinctive group practices and cultures as objects of study has enabled scholars to do the things that scholars do. Just as the fate of the Negro during the twentieth century as an object of public policy and social programs had been determined largely by scholarly and intellectual practices, so have these same practices been largely dependent on the emergence and persistence of the Negro.

Writing for the *Voice of the Negro* in 1904, Du Bois observed that if sociology was ever going to realize its goal of reconciling theory and practice in creating a science of human action, it would have to refine its focus. "The careful exhaustive study of the isolated group then is the ideal of the sociologist of the twentieth century." Accordingly, Du Bois avers,

There lies before the sociologist of the United States a peculiar opportunity. We have here going on before our eyes the evolution of a vast group of men from simpler primitive conditions to higher more complex civilization. I think it may safely be asserted that never in the history of the modern world has there been presented to men of a great nation so rare an opportunity to observe and measure and study the evolution of a great branch of the human race as is given to Americans in the study of the American Negro. . . . [All sociological] questions can be studied and answered in the case of the American Negro.[30]

By accident and design, the Negro in the United States demonstrated that humanity could be constituted as a sociological subject and that careful collection of data coupled with close observation of a specific group could move social science further toward its goal of making human beings knowable to one another.

On this point, Park concurred with Du Bois. Although his admiration for Booker T. Washington often led him to disparage Du Bois, his vision of the Negro as the sociological subject par excellence tracked almost perfectly with the lines that Du Bois had marked out in 1904. Inadvertently echoing Du Bois, Park writes, that through studying the progress of the Negro he "became convinced, finally, that I was observing a historical process by which civilization, not merely here but elsewhere, has evolved, drawing into the circle of its influence an ever-widening circle of races and peoples."[31] The Negro was distinct, different, and yet in his capacity for development like the rest of humanity.

The sociological view of the Negro as different but the same (or different but potentially the same) created for its literary critics an uncertain target. Was the central problem what the invisible man calls a "passion for conformity"[32] underwritten by the evolutionary assimilationism of sociological theory? Or was the problem embodied in such phrases as "the lady of races," which tended to overstate and make permanent the differences between the Negro and the rest of society? The invisible man's passionate insistence on the truth of the national motto "Our fate is to become one yet many" is only an artful restatement of the dilemma. His words simply take a sociological question (How can humanity be at once the same and different?) and reformulate it both as a fact ("This is not prophecy but description") and a political program

("Diversity is the word. Let man keep his many parts and you'll have no tyrant states").

The invisible man's words and Ladner's inclusion of Ellison's work in her anthology are evidence that Ellison's position did not call for a scorched-earth policy against sociology. At its lower frequencies, Ellison's commitment to diversity entailed a commitment to more refined and politically adept scholarship. The creation of a better world does not require that, first, we kill all sociologists, but rather that social scientists as a group bring to the discussion and study of the Negro the same care and sophistication that governed their study of other social groups. The questions Ellison asks at the beginning of "The World and the Jug" bear repeating here. He wonders why it is

> that when critics confront the American as *Negro* they suddenly drop their advanced critical armament and revert with an air of confident superiority to quite primitive modes of analysis? Why is that sociology-oriented critics seem to rate literature so far below politics and ideology that they would rather kill a novel than modify their presumptions concerning a given reality which it seeks in its own terms to project? Finally, why is it that so many of those who would tell us the meaning of Negro life never bother to learn how varied it really is?[33]

Answering these various questions had been the task of such essays as "The World and the Jug" and "The Little Man at Chehaw Station." In these essays Ellison responds to his own queries by asserting that most social analyses produce distorted and inadequate conclusions because researchers not only fail to take into account black culture, but they also fail to reckon on "the dispersal of ideas, styles, or tastes in this turbulent American society."[34] As illustrated by the imagery and tropes (the jug, the little man) that Ellison used in many of his essays, he believed the Negro's physical isolation could not be taken as a reliable indicator of his knowledge, sensibilities, or proclivities. His point was that despite the best efforts of segregationists, the goods of the world's culture had been available to the Negro and had played a role in shaping his tastes and sensibilities. Likewise, and equally important, the Negro, despite his segregation, had been a powerful force in creating American culture as well as the culture of the modern world. The study of the Negro, then, could not be carried out in isolation from the broader currents of American life.

This observation, however, does not answer the question as to whether a proper assessment of the Negro and modern American life required something more than being open to the unavoidably mixed-up character of American culture. Was a new mode of analysis demanded? In *"An American Dilemma*: A Review," Ellison insists, "It will take a deeper science than Myrdal's, deep as that might be, to analyze what is happening among the masses of Negroes. Much of it is inarticulate, and Negro scholars have for the most part ignored it through clinging, as does Myrdal, to the sterile concept of 'race.'" Was Ellison calling for a new science that could understand the idea of a Negro culture possessing "great value and richness, which, because it has been secreted by living and has made their lives more meaningful, Negroes will not willingly disregard"? The conclusion of Ellison's review of *An American Dilemma* is a poignant echo of Du Bois's turn-of-the-century ruminations: first, create the consciousness of the Negro, and then you will help "create a more human American."[35]

By the late 1970s, though, in such essays as "The Little Man at Chehaw Station," Ellison's new science seemed to be in large measure a reiteration of the idea of the "melting pot." One of Ellison's most frequently cited essays, "Chehaw Station" begins with an autobiographical sketch of an episode that occurred while Ellison was studying trumpet playing at Tuskegee Institute. Chastised by one of his instructors, Hazel Harrison, for trying to cover with finesse his inadequate preparation of an examination piece, Ellison is told that American reality demands that no matter where he happens to be playing, he should always perform as if even the most down-at-the-heels individual within earshot knows the tradition of the music being performed. Subtitled "The American Artist and His Audience," the essay unfolds with a series of reflections on the democratic implications of American society. Unpredictability and incongruity stand out as the hallmarks of the American experience, ideas that Ellison drives home by punctuating his reflections with an array of images—"a white youngster who, with a transistor radio screaming a Stevie Wonder tune glued to his ear, shouts racial epithets at black youngsters trying to swim at a public beach"; and an outlandishly dressed, racially ambiguous man emerging from a Volkswagen Beetle to take a series of self-portraits—that stress the unreadability of individuals. The essay then concludes with another autobiographical vignette in which Ellison recounts an unsettling but illustrative incident that occurred when he circulated a petition as a worker for the Federal Writers' Project during the depression. Finding himself standing outside a door in a tenement in San Juan Hill, Ellison hears "male Afro-American voices, raised in violent argument."[36] He pauses for a moment—not because of the belligerent voices, but because these voices are arguing vehemently "over which of two celebrated Metropolitan Opera divas was the superior soprano." How, he wonders, could these apparently uncouth coal heavers have learned enough about opera to argue knowledgeably over the talents of virtuoso sopranos? Once he steps inside the basement room, however, the mystery quickly unravels: the coal heavers tell him that they had also on occasion served as extras at the Met—"Strip us fellows down and give us some costumes and we make about the finest damn bunch of Egyptians you ever seen."[37]

"The Little Man at Chehaw Station" clearly insists on the impossibility of fixing individuals within a single tradition. In fact, Ellison interpreted the nation's growing embrace of racial and ethnic identities during the 1970s as a reaction against the loneliness of modern living. Faced with the realities described by David Riesman's *The Lonely Crowd*, Americans had, according to Ellison, grasped on to fictions of racial and ethnic affiliation for consolation and solace.[38] The American scene was fluid, ever changing, and disorienting. It was, to use one of Ellison's favorite words, "democratic" as a culture, if not as a political fact. Ellison's United States was a society in which the sociology of the group would always prove to be misleading because of the unpredictability of individual experiences and tastes. Someone would always turn out be something other than what he or she was expected to be.

Even so, by the 1980s Houston Baker and Henry Louis Gates had appropriated the vernacular origins of Ellison's little man in order to claim the "sui generis" development of an African American literary tradition. According to Baker, although Ellison intended "to advocate a traditional 'melting pot' ideal in American 'high art,' [his] observations ultimately valorize a comprehensive, vernacular expressiveness in America."[39] Inspired by Baker's reading, Gates, in turn, recasts the little man of Ellison's essay as the black cultural expert whose office was to keep the academic critic honest to his vernacular roots as he sought to apply vernacular principles to the reading of high literary texts.[40] The little man—whose role for Ellison was to chastise those "high cultural" performers who condescended to provincial audiences on the assumption that such audiences lacked the sophistication and knowledge to understand a virtuoso performance—had been transformed through a celebration of the black vernacular. Now he was a guarantor of black authenticity. For vernacular critics, keeping the little man in mind was a way to ensure that wherever the scholar happened to wander in the realms of academic criticism and theory, his readings of literary texts would remain unmistakably "black." The interpretations supplied by Baker and Gates (Gates, in particular) fueled a 1980s canon-building enterprise that insisted on the integrity of a black tradition. So that at a moment when literary theory in the academy insisted on undermining the idea of stable identities, stable meanings, and stable texts, black scholars could still produce a black canon made incarnate through major anthologies. At the end of the day, despite the poststructuralist storm raging in English departments, the Negro and his tradition remained standing.

The critical temper of that moment, which sanctioned challenges to authorial intention, played a role in legitimizing Baker's and Gates's willful misreadings of "Chehaw Station." Yet because Ellison's essay collections had not sought vigorously to smooth out his various contradictions, little ingenuity was required—if one took his corpus as a whole—to produce an Ellison often at odds with himself. If one simply wanted to expose the incompleteness of any particular construction of "Ralph Ellison," all that would have been required was a no-frills consideration of the published work. What interested vernacular critics, however, was not the multiplicity of Ellisons but the "real" Ellison behind the mask, so that while Baker notes tensions between what he calls "Ellison the merchant," whose critical utterances validate Western canonical authors, and "Ellison the creative genius," who values the black expressiveness of the blues, the two personas are hardly equal. The former was a distorting "mask" placed over the latter, which was Ellison's "genuine" self. Baker's rereading of Ellison's impassioned plea for the melting-pot ideal in "The Little Man at Chehaw Station" as a validation of the black tradition was an attempt to arrest those deconstructive energies that sought at every turn to destabilize utterances and expose their necessary incoherence. Once these energies were arrested, Ellison, to quote Baker, would always find "his most meaningful identity [in] his Afro-American self."[41]

That self, although experienced through "acts of expressive creativity," was not guaranteed only aesthetically but again, as in Gates's *Signifying Monkey*, socioeconomically. As was the case with Gates, Baker's vernacular theory rested on the presumed reality of William Julius Wilson's underclass underwriting black experience. According to Baker, Ellison, his fictional sharecropper Jim Trueblood, and by implication all black Americans were "but constituencies of a single underclass" lacking few resources other than their own creativity and expressiveness.[42] As Adolph Reed notes, Baker's vernacular arguments drew "on the standard litany of 'underclass' pundits, invoking the 'spiraling rates of teenaged pregnancies in today's black inner cities,' female-headed households, and [the] 'collapse of the black family.' "[43]

That Baker adduces all the usual sociological indices of black pathology is hardly accidental. In *Blues, Ideology, and Afro-American Literature*, he takes on Ellison in order "to demonstrate that sociology, anthropology, economics, politics, and ideology all provide models essential for the explication of the Trueblood episode,"[44] the story of Ellison's hapless sharecropper, who in a dream commits incest with his daughter, Matty Lou. Trueblood's sins transform him into a vaguely mythic figure condemned to repeat the narrative of his transgression and his retributive disfigurement at the hands of his wife, Kate. Baker's reading of the episode—which draws on Freud's *Totem and Taboo*, Clifford Geertz's "Deep Play: Notes on the Balinese Cockfight," and Victor Turner's *The Forest of Symbols*—proves to be something of a tour de force in which he proves quite adept at attending to the myriad details of the episode, deciphering Trueblood's dream in suggestively Freudian terms. Despite Baker's success, his critique nonetheless manages to unfold as a Moynihanesque remedy for black impoverishment, for when all is said and done, the reinstatement of the father as breadwinner and head of the household is the necessary prelude to black prosperity. Highlighting Ellison's description of Trueblood as a " 'hard worker' who takes care of 'his family's needs,' " Baker makes Trueblood and his family figures for the race as a whole: "His family may, in a very real sense, be construed as the entire clan, or tribe, of Afro-America."[45]

To be sure, Baker is quite sensitive to the sharecropper's plight and finds in Trueblood's words "an affirmation of a still recognizable humanity by a singer who has incorporated his personal disaster into a code of blues meanings emanating from an unpredictably chaotic world." But as insistent as Baker is in asserting Trueblood's humanity, he is even more insistent in asserting Trueblood's (and black America's) difference from the "stable, predictable, puritanical, productive, law-abiding self of the American industrial-capitalist society."[46] The problem is not Baker's critique of the normative self of "industrial-capitalist society," but his certainty that black Americans lie fully outside those norms. While white Americans might expectedly feel angst in "response to being treated as a commodity," blacks respond to that experience differently. Blacks are necessarily performers, who find "expressive representation" their only way of "negotiating a passage beyond this underclass" without compromising the integrity of their essential selves.[47] To travel from Robert Park's Negro, whose "metier" is expression, to Baker's Afro-American, whose ontology is "expressive representation," is to have moved almost without having moved at all.[48]

Invisible Man at Fifty

In late 1958 the *Saturday Review* published Ellison's "As the Spirit Moves Mahalia," a review of several recent recordings by the gospel singer Mahalia Jackson. The review is brief, and for the most part deeply appreciative; Ellison rhapsodizes, "No singer living has a greater ability to move us, regardless of our own religious attitudes, with the projected emotion of a song."[1] Mahalia Jackson was in a class by herself.

Ellison's praise, however, is not unstinting. Commenting on the singer's appearance the previous July at the Newport Jazz Festival, where she performed "Come Sunday" with the Duke Ellington Orchestra (the performance was included on one of the recordings that Ellison reviewed), Ellison laments the result as "a most unfortunate marriage and an error of taste." The gospel diva had been "given words of such banality that for all the fervor of her singing and the band's excellent performance, that Sunday sun simply would not arise. . . . [I]t was impossible for Mahalia to release that vast fund of emotion with which Southern Negroes have charged the scenes and symbols of the Gospels." The culprit for the performance's shortcoming, however, was not primarily the lyrics but the setting. Mahalia Jackson, as Ellison depicts her, is a "high priestess," whose work fully comes alive only in the context of the Negro church "because the true function of her singing is not simply to entertain, but to prepare the congregation for the minister's message, to make it receptive to the spirit, and with effects of voice and rhythm to evoke a shared community of experience."

Secular settings and recordings are merely "the next best thing," for those who "cannot, or will not, visit Mahalia in her proper setting."[2]

That Ellison was writing about a living, breathing performer meant that he did not have to face directly the historical question implicit in his argument. For him, the real Mahalia could always return to the church, and the committed listener could, if he or she wished, follow her there to join the "fortunate few" watching her perform in her proper setting. This possibility, however, said nothing about the future, when all that remained would be the electronic record. What, then, would happen to the possibility of appreciating the "real" Mahalia Jackson? Would the less-than-fortunate many, unable to visit Mahalia in her sacred setting, have to make do with nothing but a faint copy of the vibrant original?

In many ways, the obvious answer to the latter question is "Yes." Sound recordings are not the original performance. Neither, of course, are the musical scores on which performances are based. Musical performance in general is relatively time-bound. No matter how much we value our recordings, we still hunger for live performances, to be there as the music is being played. To miss the performance is to lose something irretrievable. So Mahalia's situation here was presumably no different from that of any performer. Ellison, though, was insistent on something peculiarly sacred about Jackson's authenticity. And he was far from alone in commenting on the importance of a sacred setting for Mahalia's voice. The singer herself and a large number of others agreed that watching her perform in church was a singular experience. Even Studs Terkel, who was responsible for making Mahalia Jackson a presence on Chicago radio, remarked that "watching her in a church . . . was something to experience."[3]

And yet by 1958, when Ellison wrote his review, Mahalia Jackson was an old hand with mass media outlets, studio recordings, and secular venues. She had already loosed the power of her voice in support of the Montgomery bus boycott, thus helping to galvanize the modern Civil Rights movement. And she would do so again at the 1963 March on Washington. So that while it may have been appealing for the gospel aficionado to believe that the essence of a Mahalia Jackson performance was untranslatable from its original role as part of a Sunday morning service, the varied career of gospel's first diva suggested otherwise. The growing availability of Mahalia Jackson's performances through a variety of media gave a rearguard aspect to Ellison's attempt to fix the "real" Mahalia Jackson in the sacred setting of the Negro church. Ellison's review of Mahalia also seems to fly in the face of the representation of black sacred music in *Invisible Man*. Recalling again the moment when the old man sings at Tod Clifton's funeral, the effect on the crowd is deep and authentic. Although the old man intones a spiritual rather than a gospel, the point is the same: the sacred song manages to find its place outside of a sacred setting. Even though most of those "massed together had never shared" the experiences of a Negro church, they "all were touched." The words "were all the same old slave-borne words; it was as though he'd changed the emotion beneath the words while yet the old longing, resigned, transcendent emotion still sounded above."[4] In light of the fact that five years after the publication of Ellison's review, Mahalia Jackson would sing memorably on the Washington Mall before Martin Luther King Jr.'s "I Have a Dream Speech," the novel seems prescient in its presentation of a music whose power cannot be confined to its sacred setting. Indeed, the "frequencies" of *Invisible Man* as a novel, and of many of Ellison's essays and autobiographical remarks, rely on the expectation that culture's deep meanings could be effectively transmitted from places of original performance to audiences in the most unlikely of locations. The possibility that aesthetic expertise could exist behind the stove at Chehaw Station depends on this transmission, whether through radio, recordings, or musical scores. The idea that those listeners who lacked access to the original performance venues were destined to remain less knowledgeable than those who had did have access cut against the grain of many of Ellison's published remarks.

Ellison's insistence that full appreciation of Mahalia Jackson required proper consideration of "the frame within which she moves"[5] was less a historical argument than a cultural/experiential claim more properly suited to music than to written literature. For if one element distinguishes written literature from musical recordings, it is the latter's relation (real or imagined) to the event of performance that makes the difference. Even when fully aware that a song has been recorded at different moments, track by track, listeners still tend to maintain a sense of an original moment of performance in which the sounds we are hearing have already had their first hearing by others. Granted that literature may present itself as a record of events, it is still the case that poems and novels do not generally depend on evoking the moment they came into being as aesthetic objects. Written literature, especially novels, are built for consumption at a distance. Authorial readings, even when given while the work is still in process, are ancillary to, or provide enrichment of, the work as a whole. Rarely, though, do they stand as the imagined point of origin.

One exception to this observation is the novel we currently know as *Juneteenth*. While portions of Ellison's novel-in-progress had been published during his lifetime, the second novel existed, particularly after a fire in Plainsfield reportedly destroyed much of the manuscript, primarily through the testimony of Ellison's close associates—Albert Murray, Saul Bellow, Stanley Crouch, and the late Leon Forrest—who had read segments or had heard Ellison read from the manuscript. The rumors of a book to rival or surpass *Invisible Man* hovered loudly in the air as Ellison worked unsuccessfully to bring the novel to a conclusion. And since the appearance of *Juneteenth*, these rumors have operated to create a sense of a work only imperfectly captured in the posthumous book we now have through John Callahan's editing. The true performance of what was intended to be Ellison's second novel exists in the experiences of a coterie of Ellison's associates; for the rest of us, there is presumably only this very imperfect transcript of something that—to those who were fortunate enough to catch a glimpse of it—had been an inimitable performance.[6]

The plot of *Juneteenth*, perhaps inadvertently, re-creates this tension between tour-de-force vocal performance and imperfect recording. Much of the narrative is conveyed through a joint act of reminiscence by Senator Bliss Sunraider and his mentor the Reverend Hickman in a hospital room where the senator lies wounded after having been shot on the Senate floor for his race-baiting behavior. In an attempt to redeem and understand Bliss, Hickman encourages his former protégé to recollect and reflect on his life. Bliss obliges and is soon recounting one of his stints as an itinerant preacher, when he delivered a sermon in the style of a quasi-mythical preacher named the Reverend Eatmore. Eatmore, we are told, readily mixes the homespun and the erudite in his attempt to work his spell on his listeners. Hickman is fascinated to learn that Bliss had invoked Eatmore, and he encourages the senator not only to recall the substance of the sermon but to perform it on the spot. The senator, understandably nonplussed, wonders how to do this given that he lacks all of the surroundings that presumably contribute to the success of his performance. (The reader, incredulous, wonders how one can ask a severely wounded man to deliver a sermon, even if in a whisper.) And Sunraider asks himself: "Where are the old ones to inspire me? Where are the amen corner and old exhorters, the enviable shouting sister with the nervous foot tapping out the agitation on which my voice could ride?[7] "

But Hickman is persistent and manages to prevail over the senator's misgivings by starting off the sermon himself. After a few paragraphs, Bliss then launches into the recollection, an effort that we are led to believe is successful because of Hickman's approving responses: "Ha! Now that was a true Eatmore line, Bliss. Preach it." And preach it Bliss does. Yet because Ellison's readers have not heard a true Eatmore line, we are obliged to take Hickman's word for the accuracy of the performance. Ellison's novel sets for itself the almost insurmountable task of re-creating the preacherly voice in its sacred setting through an act of recall that can only testify to, but not convey fully the power of the original. The result is a story that merely vouches for the power of black sacred voices but can never quite bring them within reach of the narrative. In the instance of Bliss's performance of Eatmore, for example, the novel seems almost self-consciously to admit its own failure when Hickman, despite his general praise of Bliss's mimicry, notes that the senator's rendition was imperfect: it had "been a long time and you smoothed up [Eatmore's] style a bit."[8] It was as if Ellison had undertaken in *Juneteenth* to prove that the novel, like Mahalia's singing, could serve the "true function" of preparing "the congregation for the minister's message," only to discover again and again that novels, unlike gospel songs, were not a part of the liturgy.[9]

Invisible Man, to be sure, owes much of its success to Ellison's ability to evoke the power of the black public voice whether through the speeches given by the unnamed preacher of the "Blackness of Blackness" sermon in the novel's prologue, the lengthy founder's day oration by the Reverend Homer A. Barbee, Ras the Exhorter's appeal to Tod Clifton, or the various speeches by the protagonist himself. Each is for a time able to work his magic on his auditors, seducing and confusing them, as does the Reverend Barbee, whose sermon on the founder moves the audience to tears, provoking "sniffing throughout the chapel." Seated with the others, the invisible man hears around him "voices murmured with admiration," and he feels "more lost than ever," having committed a blunder that he knows will lead to his exile from Barbee's vision. The mesmerizing sermon and the emotional congregation are, of course, part of an ironic setup: the voice that enables the invisible man to "see the vision" of the southern college ideal belongs to a man with "sightless eyes" (133).

As a novel, *Invisible Man* proceeds by allowing its multiple voices to reach their fullest amplitudes, only to deflate them with irony or demystification as signified by such details as Barbee's complete—and Brother Jack's partial—blindness, or by the invisible man's inability to control the effect of his own words. The spear that ripped "through both cheeks" of Ras the Exhorter and "locked his jaws" is a graphic example of the force the novel must use to silence the voices that seek to arouse and speak for the masses (560).

The novel's most potent weapon against the voices that claimed to know Negro reality, however, is the Negro himself, or "Mose," as Ellison affectionately called him in his correspondence, who could always be counted on to be different from and more complicated than the images of him that others took to be true. A legally Jim Crow America was a nation in which Mose's complexity and humanity always came as a surprise; and Ellison's novel and his literary criticism were attempts to make it clear that Mose was seeking a society in which Negro humanity could be assumed and taken for granted. In such a world, though, the problem of the Negro would necessarily look different than it had in the past. As Ellison admitted to Robert Penn Warren in *Who Speaks for the Negro?*:

> One of our problems is going to be that of affirming those things which we love about Negro life when there is no longer pressure upon us from the outside. Then the time will come when our old ways of life will say, "Well, all right, you're no longer kept within a Jim Crow community, what are you going to do about your life now? Do you think there is going to be a way of enjoying yourself which is absolutely better, more human than what you've known?"[10]

The questions posed here are not coming from "outside" the Negro experience but rather from "inside" of it. Moreover, as Ellison frames these questions, the Negro is being queried by none other than his culture: will there be a future experience so much more human than what has gone before, that it will be worth the trade of one's "old ways of life"? Having spent his career as a writer insisting that the universals of human experience were always there to be found in the experience of the Negro if one would only look, Ellison didn't believe that such a trade was necessary. The cultural world he sought would be eclectic, plural, and, because of its pluralism, recognizably Negro.

For half a century, *Invisible Man* has been one of the things that many of us have loved about Negro life. Its lyrical power and imaginative breadth have made it one of those books that we can imagine continuing to love "when there is no longer pressure upon us from the outside" to do so. There is, however, no denying the outside pressure on Ellison or how fully engaged his novel was with the political, intellectual, and moral implications of a society firmly committed to racial segregation. If Ellison found something universal in the experiences of his nameless narrator, he did so only in terms of the specific complex that was the nation's race problem. When asked in 1955 if he thought *Invisible Man* would be around twenty years after its publication, Ellison remarked:

> I doubt it. It's not an important novel. I failed of eloquence, and many of the important issues are rapidly fading away. If it does last, it will be simply because there are things going on in its depths that are of more permanent interest than on its surface. I hope so anyway.[11]

Now, more than fifty years after its publication, *Invisible Man* is still around. And while it might be tempting to attribute the novel's longevity to those things of permanent interest going on beneath the narrative's surface, the foregoing pages have suggested that it is still too early to tell because unfortunately many issues that should long ago have faded away are very much with us.

The marvel of Ellison was his having written a novel to rival the most significant fictions of the twentieth century and his having found in a world so heavily stacked against the Negro such an expansive voice. This achievement, as many scholars have reminded us, was also the marvel of spirituals, blues, jazz, and gospel—expressive forms that have ever reminded us that the people who created them were human in a way that a racially segregated white society had been unable to fathom. One wonders, though, how much longer will such reminders be necessary.

For as we work to even the odds created by a Jim Crow past, we are working, no matter what we tell ourselves, to make Ellison's novel more a story of the world that was, and less an account of the world that still is. Success here just might be a bad thing for *Invisible Man*, but such a success would be a marvelous thing, indeed.

NOTES ···························

Introduction

1. Ralph Ellison, letter to Morteza D. Sprague, May 19, 1954. Rpt. in "'American Culture Is of a Whole': From the Letters of Ralph Ellison," ed. John F. Callahan, *New Republic* 220, no. 9 (March 1, 1999): 34–49.

2. Ralph Ellison, *Invisible Man* (1952; reprint, New York: Vintage, 1990), p. 116.

3. Nathan A. Scott Jr., "Ellison's Vision of Communitas," *Carleton Miscellany: A Review of Literature and the Liberal Arts* 28, no. 3 (winter 1980): 41.

4. Ralph Ellison, introduction to *Shadow and Act*, in *The Collected Essays of Ralph Ellison*, ed. John F. Callahan (New York: Modern Library, 1995), p. 56.

5. Anna Julia Cooper, *A Voice from the South* (1892; New York: Oxford University Press, 1988).

6. See, for example, James Baldwin, "Everybody's Protest Novel," in *Notes of a Native Son* (Boston: Beacon Press, 1984), pp. 13–23; and Ralph Ellison, "The World and the Jug," in *Collected Essays*, esp. pp. 185–87.

7. Ralph Ellison, "Society, Morality and the Novel," in *Collected Essays*, p. 696.

8. Ibid., p. 697.

9. Ibid., p. 696.

10. Morris Dickstein, *Leopards in the Temple: The Transformation of American Fiction, 1945–1970* (Cambridge: Harvard University Press, 2002), p. 20.

11. Ellison, "Society, Morality and the Novel," p. 699.

12. Walter Benjamin, "Theses on the Philosophy of History," in *Illuminations*, ed. Hannah Arendt (New York: Schocken, 1969), p. 256.

13. Alexis de Tocqueville, *Democracy in America*, vol. 2, ed. Phillips Bradley (New York: Vintage Books, 1945), p. 89.

14. Chapters XIII–XIX of *Democracy in America* consider the effect of democracy on a variety of literary forms. The novel is not among them.

15. Henry James Jr., *The American Scene* (Bloomington: Indiana University Press, 1968), p. 139.

16. Frantz Fanon, *The Wretched of the Earth*, trans. Constance Farrington (New York: Grove, 1963), p. 243.

17. Amiri Baraka, *Black Music* (New York: William Morrow, 1967), esp. pp. 188–211.

18. Ralph Ellison, "Change the Joke and Slip the Yoke," in *Collected Essays,* p. 109.

19. Ralph Ellison, *Juneteenth: A Novel* (New York: Random House, 1999), n.p.

20. The nostalgia I'm criticizing includes such works as Henry Louis Gates's *Colored People: A Memoir* (New York: Knopf, 1994), and Clifton Taulbert's novel *Once upon a Time When We Were Colored* (Tulsa: Council Oak Books, 1989), which was made into a feature film by Tim Reid. To this list I would add the social theory of William Julius Wilson, which tends to represent the racially segregated neighborhoods of Jim Crow America as a period of communal stability: "Though they may have lived on different streets, blacks of all classes in inner-city areas such as Bronzeville lived in the same community and shopped at the same stores. Their children went to the same schools and played in the same parks. Although there was some degree of class antagonism, their neighborhoods were more stable than the inner-city neighborhoods of today." See William Julius Wilson, foreword to *Black Metropolis: A Study of Negro Life in a Northern City*, by St. Clair Drake and Horace R. Cayton (Chicago: University of Chicago Press, 1993), p. xlix. For a succinct critique of this trend, see Adolph Reed Jr., "Romancing Jim Crow," in *Class Notes: Posing as Politics and Other Thoughts on the American Scene* (New York: New Press, 2000), pp. 14–24.

21. David Harvey, *Justice, Nature and the Geography of Difference* (Malden, Mass.: Blackwell, 1996), p. 40. Harvey goes on to draw a problematic analogy between working-class movements and women in abusive relationships, observing, "Working-class movements may then seek to perpetuate or return to the conditions of oppression that spawned them in much the same way that those women who have acquired their sense of self under conditions of male violence return again and again to living with violent men." Harvey may err on both sides of the analogy in stressing "sense of self" as the reason for the return to oppressive conditions. Women tend to return to abusive relationships as a result of a perceived and real lack of alternatives, lack of resources, fear of further violence, etc. Social movements return to tried-and-true appeals to solidarity because there appear to be plenty of reasons to believe that what worked in the past will likely work in the future.

It's also worth pointing out that Harvey's remedy for the problem of working-class conservatism is not to abandon "class politics for those of the 'new social movements,' but the exploration of different forms of alliances that can reconstitute and renew class politics." The danger here is that Harvey focuses too much on the "who," i.e., how can working-class whites form allegiances with inner-city blacks, and not enough on the "what," e.g., why we should all support free and equal access to health care and education.

22. Robin D. G. Kelley, *Race Rebels: Culture, Politics, and the Black Working Class* (New York: Free Press, 1994), p. 181; Michael Eric Dyson, *I May Not Get There with You: The True Martin Luther King, Jr.* (New York: Free Press, 2000), p. 177.

23. Dyson, *I May Not Get There with You*, p. 178.

24. To be sure, accounts of black leadership tend to include caveats that the demands of the present differ from those of the past. For example, Cornel West writes, "The time is past for black political and intellectual leaders to pose as *the* voice for black America. Gone are the days when black political leaders jockey for the label 'president of black America,' or when black intellectuals pose as the 'writers of black America.' " Nonetheless, in the same paragraph, West rescues the notion of black leadership that he has just dismissed: "To be a serious black leader is to be a race-transcending prophet." See Cornel West, *Race Matters* (Boston: Beacon Press, 1993), p. 46. For a critique of the inadvertent hagiographic tendencies in black political commentary of the 1980s and 1990s, see Adolph Reed, *W. E. B. Du Bois and American Political Thought: Fabianism and the Color Line* (New York: Oxford University Press, 1997), pp. 177–86.

25. Kenneth Burke, "Ralph Ellison's Trueblooded *Bildungsroman*," in *Speaking for You: The Vision of Ralph Ellison*, ed. Kimberley W. Bentson (Washington, D.C.: Howard University Press, 1987), p. 350; Dickstein, *Leopards in the Temple*, p. 19.

26. Walter Benn Michaels, *Our America: Nativism, Modernism, and Pluralism* (Durham, N.C.: Duke University Press, 1995), p. 13.

27. Ibid., p. 139.

28. Ralph Ellison, "Twentieth-Century Fiction and the Black Mask of Humanity," in *Collected Essays*, p. 88.

29. Ellison, "The World and the Jug," p. 186.

30. Ellison, "Society, Morality and the Novel," p. 709.

31. *Plessy* v. *Ferguson*, 163 U.S. 537. Decision by Justice Henry Billings Brown, May 18, 1896.

32. William Graham Sumner, *Folkways; a Study of the Sociological Importance of Usages, Manners, Customs, Mores, and Morals*, with a special introduction by William Lyon Phelps (New York: Dover, 1959), p. 77.

33. Ellison to Senator Abraham Ribicoff, Testimony for the U.S. Senate Subcommittee Investigation, "Federal Role in Urban Problems," *New Leader* 49, no. 19 (September 26, 1966): 24.

34. Ellison, "Twentieth-Century Fiction and the Black Mask of Humanity," p. 98.

35. Ellison, "Society, Morality and the Novel," p. 722. Ellison also chided Malcolm Cowley's *The Portable Faulkner*—the text that had helped establish Faulkner's literary reputation—for allowing readers to believe that they could skip that section of "The Bear" if they wanted to read "one of the greatest [hunting stories] in the language" (quoted in Ellison, "Society, Morality and the Novel," p. 721).

36. William Faulkner, "The Bear," in *Go Down, Moses* (New York: Modern Library, 1995), pp. 277–78.

37. Ulrich Bonnell Phillips, preface to *American Negro Slavery: A Survey of the Supply, Employment and Control of Negro Labor as Determined by the Plantation Regime* (1918; reprint, Baton Rouge: Louisiana State University Press, 1966), n.p.

38. Ellison, letter to Albert Murray, March 16, 1956, in *Trading Twelves: The Selected Letters of Ralph Ellison and Albert Murray*, ed. John F. Callahan (New York: Modern Library, 2000), p. 117.

39. Shelley Fisher Fishkin, *Was Huck Black? Mark Twain and African American Voices* (New York: Oxford University Press, 1993), pp. 134, 143.

40. Stanley Crouch, "The Oklahoma Kid," *New Republic* 210, no. 19 (May 9, 1994): 23.

41. Arthur M. Schlesinger Jr., *The Disuniting of America* (New York: W. W. Norton, 1991), p. 91.

42. Sean Wilentz, quotation confirmed via e-mail, February 6, 2003.

43. Norman Podhoretz, "What Happened to Ralph Ellison," *Commentary* 108, no. 1 (July/August 1999): 46–58. Podhoretz's bill of particulars tells us much more about Podhoretz's politics and prejudices than about *Invisible Man* and its current literary reputation. And Podhoretz's complaints seem driven largely by his never having quite forgiven Ellison for failing to respond to his 1963 article "My Negro Problem—and Ours." Podhoretz writes, "Yet in at least two discussions I had with him about the piece—discussions he was so reluctant to enter that I had to prod him out of his loud silence by asking flatly where he stood in the heated controversy my essay had generated—he said nothing to me about the insult I had hurled at the culture of the American Negro" (56).

44. Ibid., p. 58.

45. Shelby Steele, "The Content of His Character," *New Republic* 220, no. 9 (March 1, 1999): 29.

46. Quoted in David Remnick, "Visible Man," *New Yorker* 70, no. 4 (March 14, 1994): 38

47. Harold Cruse, *The Crisis of the Negro Intellectual* (New York: Quill, 1984), p. 509.

48. Larry Neal, "The Black Writer's Role, II: Ellison's Zoot Suit," in *Visions of a Liberated Future: Black Arts Movement Writings* (New York: Thunder's Mouth Press, 1989), p. 41.

49. Houston A. Baker Jr., *Blues, Ideology, and Afro-American Literature* (Chicago: University of Chicago Press, 1984).

50. Ellison, "The World and the Jug," pp. 164, 185.

51. Henry Louis Gates Jr., *Figures in Black: Words, Signs, and the Racial Self* (New York: Oxford University Press, 1988), pp. 36–37.

52. Henry Louis Gates Jr., *The Signifying Monkey* (New York: Oxford University Press, 1988), p. xxiii.

53. Ibid., p. xxii.

54. Gates, *Figures in Black*, pp. 40–41 (italics mine).

55. Henry Louis Gates et al., *The Norton Anthology of African American Literature* (New York: W. W. Norton, 1995), p. xxxvi.

56. Jerry Gafio Watts, *Heroism and the Black Intellectual* (Chapel Hill: University of North Carolina Press, 1994), p. 107.

57. Ralph Ellison, *Invisible Man* (1952; reprint, New York: Vintage, 1990), p. 581. (Subsequent references appear parenthetically in the text.)

58. Adolph Reed, *Stirrings in the Jug: Black Politics in the Post-Segregation Era* (Minneapolis: University of Minnesota Press, 1999), p. 16.

59. Irving Howe, *Politics and the Novel* (New York: Fawcett, 1947), p. 166.

60. Watts, *Heroism and the Black Intellectual*, pp. 12, 32.

61. Ellison, "Twentieth-Century Fiction and the Black Mask of Humanity," pp. 91, 92.

62. Ellison, "The World and the Jug," p. 186.

63. Ellison, "Twentieth-Century Fiction and the Black Mask of Humanity," p. 81.

64. Ralph Ellison, "Hidden Name and Complex Fate," in *Collected Essays*, p. 208.

Chapter 1

Portions of chapter 1 first appeared in an essay entitled "Ralph Ellison and the Reconfiguration of Black Cultural Poetics," in *REAL: Yearbook of Research in English and American Literature,* vol. 11, ed. W. Fluck (Tübingen: Gunter Narr Verlag, 1995).

1. Nor was it entirely right, either. Mark Twain in *Life and Times on the Mississippi* (New York: Signet, 1961) and, more recently, T. J. Jackson Lears in *No Place of Grace: Antimodernism and the Transformation of American Culture, 1880–1920* (New York: Pantheon Books, 1981), have pointed out the social and cultural power wielded by chivalric ideals through the nineteenth and into the twentieth centuries.

2. Of course, the obvious reference here is to Mikhail Bakhtin, "Discourse in the Novel," in *The Dialogic Imagination: Four Essays,* trans. Caryl Emerson and Michael Holquist (Austin: University of Texas Press, 1981), pp. 259–422. See especially Bakhtin's claim that in the comic novel the "incorporated languages and socio-ideological belief systems, while of course utilized to refract the author's intentions, are unmasked and destroyed as something false, hypocritical, greedy, limited, narrowly rationalistic, inadequate to reality" (311–12).

3. Langston Hughes, "The Negro Artist and the Racial Mountain," *Nation* 122 (June 23, 1926): 692.

4. Horace A. Porter, *Jazz Country: Ralph Ellison in America* (Iowa City: University of Iowa Press, 2001), p. 74.

5. Houston A. Baker Jr. *Blues, Ideology, and Afro-American Literature* (Chicago: University of Chicago Press, 1984), p. 13.

6. Hazel Carby, "Policing the Black Woman's Body in an Urban Context," *Critical Inquiry* 18, no. 4 (summer 1992): 754.

7. Ibid., p. 741.

8. Robin D. G. Kelley, *Race Rebels: Culture, Politics, and the Black Working Class* (New York: Free Press, 1994), p. 165.

9. W. E. B. Du Bois, *Dusk of Dawn: An Autobiography of a Race Concept,* in *Writings* (New York: Library of America, 1986), p. 761.

10. W. E. B. Du Bois, "Segregation," *Crisis* (January 1934): 20.

11. Du Bois, *Dusk of Dawn,* p. 777.

12. Jeannie M. Whayne, *A New Plantation South: Land, Labor, and Federal Favor in Twentieth-Century Arkansas* (Charlottesville: University Press of Virginia, 1996), pp. 184–85.

13. David Leering Lewis's *W. E. B. Du Bois: The Fight for Equality and the American Century, 1919–1963* (New York: Henry Holt, 2000), provides a lively account of the rift caused by Du Bois's tactical maneuvers; see especially pp. 331–48.

14. Du Bois, *Dusk of Dawn*, p. 777.

15. Quoted in Lewis, *W. E. B. Du Bois*, p. 343. Du Bois refers here to his May 1934 *Crisis* article, "The Board of Directors on Segregation," rpt. in W. E. B. Du Bois, *Writings* (New York: Library of America, 1986), pp. 1252–53.

16. W. E. B. Du Bois, *The Autobiography of W. E. B. Du Bois: A Soliloquy on Viewing My Life from the Last Decade of Its First Century* (New York: International Publishers, 1968), p. 296. On the relation of Du Bois's tactical segregation to working-class politics, see Judith Stein's review of David Levering Lewis's *W. E. B. Du Bois: The Fight for Equality and the American Century, 1919–1963* ("W. E. B. Du Bois," *Reviews in American History* 29, no. 2 [June 2001]: 247–54), and Adolph Reed's *W. E. B. Du Bois and American Political Thought*, esp. 53–70.

17. Du Bois, *Dusk of Dawn*, p. 761.

18. Ralph Ellison, "Beating That Boy," in *The Collected Essays of Ralph Ellison*, ed. John F. Callahan (New York: Modern Library, 1995), p. 148.

19. Reprinted testimony in "Harlem's America: From the U.S. Senate Investigation of the Crisis in Our Cities," *New Leader* (September 26, 1966): 24, 34.

20. Even some of the more astute critiques of the cultural turn, among them Jon Cruz's *Culture on the Margins*, contribute to naturalizing black political marginalization. While Cruz is properly attuned to the way "a peculiar kind of culturalism triumphed through a cultural eclipse of politics" during the late nineteenth and early twentieth centuries (6), he continues to define the issue as one of listening to the voices on the margin ("the people on the so-called margins of society can actually tell us much about the fateful, disastrous, or promising directions of the center" [202]). Although there is not adequate space here to attend to all of the nuances of Cruz's study, which locates the origins of contemporary cultural critique in Frederick Douglass's reading of slave singing in his 1845 *Narrative*, his inquiry participates inadvertently in valuing the period of slavery, which saw a "new politics of subjects during the height of the abolitionist movement," over the moments of emancipation, which he sees as marked by a "restricted and increasingly enclosed domain that centered upon the preferred religious expressivity of blacks, and then as its culmination in the modern bifurcation between inner knowledge and objective classification" (198). See Jon Cruz, *Culture on the Margins: The Black Spiritual and the Rise of Cultural Interpretation* (Princeton: Princeton University Press, 1999).

21. Anna Julia Cooper, *A Voice from the South* (1892; New York: Oxford University Press, 1988), p. 37.

22. Ibid. p. 36.

23. Thomas Dixon Jr., *The Clansman: An Historical Romance of the Ku Klux Klan* (Lexington: University of Kentucky Press, 1970), p. 1. The full quotation of Dixon's remarks is as follows:

> The chaos of blind passion that followed Lincoln's assassination is inconceivable to-day. The Revolution it produced in our Government, and the bold attempt of Thaddeus Stevens to Africanise ten great states of the American Union, read now like tales from "The Arabian Nights."
>
> I have sought to preserve in this romance both the letter and the spirit of this remarkable period.

24. Cooper, *A Voice from the South*, pp. 182, 181.

25. Kenneth Burke, "Ralph Ellison's Trueblooded *Bildungsroman*," in *Speaking for You: The Vision of Ralph Ellison*, ed. Kimberley W. Bentson (Washington, D.C.: Howard University Press, 1987), p. 359.

26. On Johnson's role in the Harlem Renaissance, see David Levering Lewis, *When Harlem Was in Vogue* (New York: Vintage, 1982), esp. pp. 89–100.

27. Ralph Ellison, "A Congress Jim Crow Didn't Attend," in *The Collected Essays of Ralph Ellison*, ed. John F. Callahan (New York: Modern Library" 1995), pp. 25, 26.

28. Barbara Foley, "Ralph Ellison as Proletarian Journalist," *Science & Society* 62, no. 4 (winter 1998/1999): 537. Although less adamant than Foley in asserting Ellison's 1930s and 1940s left politics, Lawrence Jackson remarks on the "materialist-inflected view" in some of Ellison's work from these decades. *Ralph Ellison: Emergence of Genius* (New York: Wiley & Son, 2002), p. 206.

29. Ralph Ellison, "*An American Dilemma*: A Review," in *The Collected Essays of Ralph Ellison*, ed. John F. Callahan (New York: Modern Library, 1995), p. 331.

30. Michel Fabre, "From *Native Son* to *Invisible Man*: Some Notes on Ralph Ellison's Evolution in the 1950s," in *Speaking for You*, ed. Bentson, p. 206. There is some critical debate on this point. Although Jerry Gafio Watts in *Heroism and the Black Intellectual* discusses Ellison's development into the heroic artist, Watts also sees this development as largely preordained: "Ellison by his very nature was not the political man that [Richard Wright] was. Wright lived for politics in much the same way that Ellison lived for culture" (43). By contrast, the anti-protest animus of Marcus Klein in *After Alienation: American Novels in Mid-Century* (Cleveland: World Publishing, 1964) leads him to see Ellison's ultimate artistic destination as having been won after considerable struggle against the claims of politics (see pp. 85–100). On Ellison's evolution, Foley observes, "The 1944 Myrdal review is often cited as evidence of Ellison's antipathy to the Communists and corroboration of the portraiture of Brotherhood manipulation in *Invisible Man*." She adds, "In my view, however, this text—which remained unpublished until 1965, for reasons not yet clear—cannot be taken as indicative of a clear break with the CP-led left" ("Ralph Ellison as Proletarian Journalist," p. 539).

31. Ellison, "*An American Dilemma*: A Review," p. 340.

32. Barbara Foley, "From Communism to Brotherhood: The Drafts of *Invisible Man*," in *Twentieth-Century Americanisms: The Left and Modern Literatures in the United States*, ed. Bill V. Mullen and James A. Smethurst (University of North Carolina Press, 2003).

33. Rayford W. Logan, *The Betrayal of the Negro: from Rutherford B. Hayes to Woodrow Wilson*, intro. Eric Foner (New York: Da Capo Press, 1997), p. 5.

34. Kobena Mercer, *Welcome to the Jungle: New Positions in Black Cultural Studies* (New York: Routledge, 1994), p. 246.

35. Paul Gilroy, *The Black Atlantic* (Cambridge: Harvard University Press, 1993), p. 40.

36. Julie Saville, *The Work of Reconstruction* (New York: Cambridge University Press, 1994), p. 114.

37. Gilroy, *The Black Atlantic*, 37. I'm taking Gilroy's arguments to be roughly representative of the cultural turn. Even the critics that Gilroy attacks most harshly share his belief in the centrality of music to black politics. Cf. Houston Baker, *Afro-American Poetics: Revisions of Harlem and the Black Aesthetic* (Madison: University of Wisconsin Press, 1988): "The black valley is communal space where the medium's work is abortive without contagious group response. The trance, in a word, is dependent upon folk sounds for its very inducement. There is a reciprocity, then, in which 'soul sounds' that hint of a racial 'genius' surpassing speech lead to the medium's entrancement. Trance produces, in turn, further sounds or songs that are, at best, metonyms for the deepest spiritual reaches of inaudible valleys" (107).

38. Saville, *The Work of Reconstruction*, p. 92.

39. Eric Foner, *Reconstruction: America's Unfinished Revolution, 1863–1877* (New York: Harper and Row, 1988), pp. 114, 291.

40. Gilroy, *The Black Atlantic*, p. 30.

41. Du Bois, *Dusk of Dawn*, p. 91.

42. James Weldon Johnson, *The Autobiography of an Ex-Coloured Man* (1912; reprint, New York: Vintage, 1989), p. 142.

43. Ibid., pp. 46, 173.

44. Ibid., pp. 3, 210, 3, 211.

45. Ralph Ellison, "Twentieth-Century Fiction and the Black Mask of Humanity," in *Collected Essays*, p. 86.

46. Ralph Ellison, "*An American Dilemma*: A Review," in *Collected Essays*, p. 306.

47. Richard Wright, *Native Son* (New York: Harper & Row, 1940), pp. 391–92.

48. W. E. B. Du Bois, *Souls of Black Folk*, in *Writings* (New York: Library of America, 1986), p. 360.

Chapter 2

1. Terry Eagleton, *Ideology: An Introduction* (New York: Verso, 1991), p. 119.

2. Ibid. To be sure, the invisible man may be only an imperfect analogue of the organic intellectual, whose "mode of being," according to Gramsci, can no longer

consist in eloquence, which is an exterior and momentary mover of feelings and passions, but in active participation in practical life, as constructor, organizer, "permanent persuader," and not just a simple orator (but superior at the same time to the abstract mathematical spirit) (10). Ellison's protagonist is nothing if not eloquent, and to the degree we want to see him standing in for the novel and at various points for the novelist, it might be truer to be speaking here of the "captured" traditional intellectual than of the organic intellectual.

3. Houston A. Baker Jr. *Critical Memory: Public Spheres, African American Writing, and Black Fathers and Sons in America* (Athens: University of Georgia Press, 2001), p. 67.

4. Benedict Anderson, *Imagined Communities: Reflections on the Origin and Spread of Nationalism*, rev. ed. (New York: Verso, 1991), p. 141.

5. Ibid., p. 9.

6. Ibid.

7. Ibid., p. 205.

8. Toni Morrison, *The Song of Solomon* (New York: Random House, 1984), p. 154.

9. Hannah Arendt, *The Human Condition* (Chicago: University of Chicago Press, 1957), p. 181.

10. Ibid., p. 55.

11. Anderson, *Imagined Communities*, p. 9.

12. Steven Lee Myers, "Scientific Advances End Rite of War 'Unknowns' at Tomb," *New York Times* (February 25, 1999), p. A1.

13. Ibid., p. A18.

14. Morrison, *Song of Solomon*, p. 155.

15. Baker's celebration of the march in *Critical Memory* was probably more to the point in proclaiming "the inseparability of message and messenger" (p. 58).

16. Eagleton, *The Ideology of the Aesthetic*, p. 181.

17. Hortense Spillers, "Mama's Baby, Papa's Maybe: An American Grammar Book," *Diacritics* (summer 1987): 65–81.

Chapter 3

1. Ralph Ellison, "If the Twain Shall Meet," in *The Collected Essays of Ralph Ellison*, ed. John F. Callahan (New York: Modern Library, 1995), p. 565.

2. Ralph Ellison, "The Myth of the Flawed White Southerner," in *Collected Essays*, pp. 554–56. I take up this essay at greater length in "As White as Anybody: Race and the Politics of Counting as Black," *New Literary History* 31, no. 4 (autumn 2000).

3. Howard Zinn, *The Southern Mystique* (New York: Knopf, 1964), p. 4.

4. Ibid., p. 13.

5. Ellison, "If the Twain Shall Meet," p. 573.

6. George Washington Cable, "Literature in the Southern States," *The Negro Question*, ed. Arlin Turner (New York: Doubleday, 1958), pp. 43, 44.

7. Ibid., pp. 38, 44.

8. Ibid., p. 43.

9. C. Vann Woodward, *The Burden of Southern History*, rev. ed. (Baton Rouge: Louisiana State University Press, 1968), p. 25.

10. Zinn, *Southern Mystique*, p. 25.

11. Ellison, "If the Twain Shall Meet," p. 574.

12. Lawrence Jackson, *Ralph Ellison: Emergence of Genius* (New York: John Wiley & Sons, 2002), p. 331.

13. Ralph Ellison, "The World and the Jug," in *Collected Essays*, pp. 187, 188.

14. Barbara Foley, *Radical Representations: Politics and Form in U.S. Proletarian Fiction, 1929–1941* (Durham: Duke University Press, 1993), p. 167.

15. Richard Wright, "Blueprint for Negro Writing," in *Richard Wright Reader*, ed. Ellen Wright and Michel Fabre (New York: Harper and Row, 1978), p. 48.

16. Robert G. O'Meally, *The Craft of Ralph Ellison* (Cambridge: Harvard University Press, 1980), p. 24.

17. Ralph Ellison, "*An American Dilemma*: A Review," in *Collected Essays*, p. 339.

18. Zinn, *Southern Mystique*, p. 265.

19. Stanley M. Elkins, *Slavery: A Problem in American Institutional and Intellectual Life* (Chicago: University of Chicago Press, 1976), p. 130.

20. Zinn, *Southern Mystique*, p. 36.

21. Ellison, "If the Twain Shall Meet," p. 573.

22. See O'Meally, *The Craft of Ralph Ellison*, pp. 23–24.

23. Ralph Ellison, "Change the Joke and Slip the Yoke," in *Collected Essays*, p. 109.

24. Ibid., p. 98.

25. Ellison, "If the Twain Shall Meet," p. 574.

26. William Graham Sumner, *Folkways; a Study of the Sociological Importance of Usages, Manners, Customs, Mores, and Morals*, with a special introduction by William Lyon Phelps (New York: Dover, 1959), p. 77.

27. Ellison, "The World and the Jug," p. 178.

28. Ralph Ellison, "What Would America Be Like without Blacks," in *Collected Essays*, p. 578.

29. Ibid., pp. 581–82.

30. W. E. B. Du Bois, *Souls of Black Folk*, in *Writings* (New York: Library of America, 1986), p. 545.

31. Malcolm X, "The Ballot or the Bullet," in *Malcolm X Speaks* (New York: Grove Weidenfeld, 1965), p. 36.

32. Elkins, *Slavery*, pp. vii, 300.

33. Ibid., pp. 274–75.

34. Ibid., p. 277 n. 10.

35. Eugene Genovese, "*Roll, Jordan, Roll": The World the Slaves Made* (New York: Vintage, 1976).

36. Elkins, *Slavery*, p. 269.

37. Ibid., p. 270.

38. Moynihan's Report, of course, had diagnosed the ills afflicting America's black citizens as deriving from a persistent consequence of the slave regime: the

structure of the black family had become matriarchal in a society in which patriarchal nuclear families defined the norm. The result was black families exhibiting all manner of pathologies—pathologies that could be remedied by a massive program of federal intervention premised on reorganizing black family structures.

39. Elkins, *Slavery*, p. 270.

40. Ibid., p. 301.

41. Ralph Ellison, "Richard Wright's Blues," in *Collected Essays*, p. 129.

42. Ibid., p. 134.

43. Ibid., pp. 136, 135.

44. Ibid., p. 131.

45. Ibid., p. 136.

46. Adolph Reed, "The Allure of Malcolm X," in *Stirrings in the Jug: Black Politics in the Post-Segregation Era* (Minneapolis: University of Minnesota Press, 1999), p. 223. Elkins, too, notes that despite their venom, nationalists seemed not to have "had any real quarrel with the actual prescriptions Moynihan envisioned" (Elkins, *Slavery*, p. 272).

47. Ellison, "Richard Wright's Blues," p. 131.

48. Jerry Gafio Watts, in *Heroism and the Black Intellectual* (Chapel Hill: University of North Carolina Press, 1994), p. 107, notes in passing Ellison's occasional echoing of Chicago school findings.

49. Daryl Michael Scott, *Contempt and Pity: Social Policy and the Image of the Damaged Black Psyche, 1880–1996* (Chapel Hill: University of North Carolina Press), p. 168. Scott's tracking of the "image of the damaged black psyche" helpfully illuminates not only the conditions that gave rise to, but also the assets and liabilities of, the damage thesis. His observations on Ellison's relation to that thesis are likewise helpful, but sometimes limited. His paraphrase of Ellison's critique of *Native Son*, "Ellison could imagine the invisible man, but the invisible man could not imagine Ralph Ellison" (168), has about it more wit than sense. The distance between character and author in Ellison's novel nowhere approaches that defining the same relation in *Native Son*.

50. Lawrence W. Levine, *Black Culture and Black Consciousness: Afro-American Folk Thought from Slavery to Freedom* (New York: Oxford University Press, 1977), p. 80.

51. Ibid., pp. 138, 283, 293, 445.

52. Ibid., pp. 444–45.

53. Ulrich Bonnell Phillips, *American Negro Slavery: A Survey of the Supply, Employment and Control of Negro Labor as Determined by the Plantation Regime* (Baton Rouge: Louisiana State University Press, 1966), p. 514.

54. Eugene Genovese, foreword to *American Negro Slavery*, by Ulrich Bonnell Phillips, p. xxi.

55. Houston Baker, *Turning South Again: Re-Thinking Modernism/Re-Reading Booker T.* (Durham, N.C.: Duke University Press, 2001), pp. 22, 98, 77–78. Ironically, Baker's recent rereadings of the south are an attempt to revise some of the views he adopted in earlier works. The crucial difference, however, is that he is

harsher on some individual writers whom he had praised earlier. The nationalist underpinnings of the work remain in place.

56. Du Bois, *Souls of Black Folk*, p. 57.

57. David Greenberg, "Sambo Returns: Were Slaves Happy? The Answer's Not as Simple as You'd Think," *Slate*, posted Thursday, November 26, 1998, http://slate.msn.com/id/9089/.

58. Also see Scott, *Contempt and Pity*, pp. 190–92, on the persistence of damage imagery among late-twentieth-century black intellectuals.

59. Eugene Rivers, "On the Responsibility of the Intellectual in the Age of Crack," *Boston Review* 20, no. 3 (September–October 1992). Posted December 20, 2002, *http://bostonreview.mit.edu/BR17.5/rivers.html*; William Julius Wilson, foreword to *Black Metropolis: A Study of Negro Life in a Northern City*, by St. Clair Drake and Horace R. Cayton (Chicago: University of Chicago Press, 1993), pp. l–li.

60. Cornel West, *Race Matters* (Boston: Beacon Press, 1993), pp. 15–16.

61. Toni Morrison, "City Limits, Village Values: Concepts of the Neighborhood in Black Fiction," in *Literature and the Urban Experience: Essays on the City and Literature*, ed. Michael C. Jaye and Ann Chalmers Watts (New Brunswick: Rutgers University Press, 1981), p. 38.

62. Cornel West, *The Ethical Dimensions of Marxist Thought* (New York: Monthly Review Press, 1991), pp. xxiv, xxxii.

63. Eugene Genovese, *The Southern Tradition: The Achievement and Limitations of an American Conservatism* (Cambridge: Harvard University Press, 1994), p. 102.

64. West, *Race Matters*, p. 19.

65. Ibid.

66. Toni Morrison, *Beloved* (New York: Plume, 1987), p. 261.

67. Ibid., pp. 152, 171.

68. Ibid., pp. 256, 261.

69. Ibid., p. 246.

70. See West, *The Ethical Dimensions of Marxist Thought*, p. xxiv.

71. Eugene Genovese, "Eugene Rivers' Challenge: A Response," *Boston Review* 21, no. 3 (September–October 1993). Posted December 20, 2002, *http://bostonreview.mit.edu/BR18.5/eugenerivers.html*; see p. x.

72. Ibid.

73. See Scott, *Contempt and Pity*, pp. 181–82.

74. Ellison, "The World and the Jug," p. 160.

75. West, *Race Matters*, pp. 16–17.

Chapter 4

1. Joyce A. Ladner, introduction to *The Death of White Sociology: Essays on Race and Culture*, ed. Joyce A. Ladner (Baltimore: Black Classic Press, 1998), p. xxviii.

2. Ibid., p. xxi.

3. John Bracey, August Meier, and Elliott Rudwick, "The Black Sociologists: The First Half Century," in *The Death of White Sociology*, ed. Ladner, p. 12.

4. Ladner, introduction to *The Death of White Sociology*, p. xxi.

5. W. E. B. Du Bois, *Souls of Black Folk*, in *Writings* (New York: Library of America, 1986), p. 368.

6. Alain Locke, "The New Negro," in *The New Negro: Voices of the Harlem Renaissance*, ed. Alain Locke (New York: Atheneum, 1992), p. 3.

7. James Baldwin, "Everybody's Protest Novel," in *Notes of a Native Son* (Boston: Beacon Press, 1984), p. 19.

8. Henry Louis Gates Jr., *Figures in Black: Words, Signs, and the Racial Self* (New York: Oxford University Press, 1988), p. 45.

9. Baldwin, "Everybody's Protest Novel," p. 19.

10. Henry Louis Gates Jr., *The Signifying Monkey* (New York: Oxford University Press, 1988), p. 46.

11. Richard Wright, introduction to *Black Metropolis: A Study of Negro Life in a Northern City*, by St. Clair Drake and Horace R. Cayton (Chicago: University of Chicago Press, 1993), p. xviii.

12. Cheryl Wall, "On Freedom and the Will to Adorn: Debating Aesthetics and/as Ideology in African American Literature," in *Aesthetics and Ideology*, ed. George Levine (New Brunswick, N.J.: Rutgers University Press, 1994), p. 290.

13. Robert Park, "The Negro as Revealed through His Literature," *Race and Culture: The Collected Papers of Robert Ezra Park*, vol. 1, ed. Everett Cherington Hughes, Charles S. Johnson et al. (Glencoe, Ill.: Free Press, 1950), pp. 284–85.

14. Ralph Ellison, "*An American Dilemma*: A Review," in *The Collected Essays of Ralph Ellison*, ed. John F. Callahan (New York: Modern Library, 1995), p. 332.

15. Gates, *Signifying Monkey*, p. 47.

16. Elizabeth Long, "Introduction: Engaging Sociology and Cultural Studies: Disciplinarity," in *From Sociology to Cultural Studies: New Perspectives*, ed. Elizabeth Long (London: Blackwell, 1997), pp. 2–3. Henry Yu's *Thinking Orientals: Migration, Contact, and Exoticism in Modern America* (New York: Oxford University Press, 2001) is also insightful on the commitment to culture in Chicago school sociology.

17. Robert Park, "An Autobiographical Statement," in *Race and Culture*, pp. vi–vii.

18. Gates, *Figures in Black*, p. 124.

19. Park, "The Negro as Revealed through His Literature," p. 300.

20. Jean Toomer, *Cane* (New York: Boni & Liveright, 1923).

21. Robert Park, "The Nature of Race Relations," in *Race and Culture*, p. 104.

22. Park, "The Negro as Revealed through His Literature," p. 294.

23. Ibid., p. 300.

24. Park, "The Nature of Race Relations," p. 104.

25. Gates, *Signifying Monkey*, p. xix.

26. William Julius Wilson, foreword to *Black Metropolis*, by Drake and Cayton, pp. l–li. Also Wilson, *The Declining Significance of Race* (Chicago: University of

Chicago Press, 1980), pp. 19–23.

27. Albert Murray, "White Norms, Black Deviation," in *The Death of White Sociology*, ed. Ladner, p. 100.

28. Adolph Reed Jr. and Larry Bennett, "The New Face of Urban Renewal: The Near North Redevelopment Initiative and the Cabrini-Green Neighborhood," in *Without Justice for All: The New Liberalism and Our Retreat from Racial Equality*, ed. Adolph Reed Jr. (Boulder: Westview Press, 1999), p. 187.

29. See Henry Louis Gates Jr., "Are We Better Off?" *Frontline*. Posted December 20, 2002, *http://www.pbs.org/wgbh/pages/frontline/shows/race/etc/gates/html*.

30. W. E. B. Du Bois, "The Atlanta Conferences," *Voice of the Negro* 1 (March 1904): 85–89; reprinted in *W.E.B. Du Bois on Sociology and the Black Community*, ed. Dan S. Green and Edwin D. Driver (Chicago: University of Chicago Press, 1978), pp. 54–55.

31. See Robert Park, "An Autobiographical Note," in *Race and Culture*, pp. vi–vii, viii.

32. Ralph Ellison, *Invisible Man* (1952; reprint, New York: Vintage, 1990), p. 577.

33. Ralph Ellison, "The World and the Jug," in *The Collected Essays of Ralph Ellison*, ed. John F. Callahan (New York: Modern Library, 1995), p. 146.

34. Ralph Ellison, "The Little Man at Chehaw Station," in *Collected Essays*, p. 495.

35. Ralph Ellison, "*An American Dilemma*: A Review," in *Collected Essays*, p. 340.

36. Ellison, "Little Man at Chehaw Station," p. 515.

37. Ibid., pp. 515, 519.

38. Ellison writes, "He is nevertheless (and by the nature of his indefinite relationship to the fluid social hierarchy) a lonely individual who must find his own way within a crowd of other lonely individuals" ("Little Man at Chehaw Station," p. 504).

39. Houston A. Baker Jr., *Blues, Ideology, and Afro-American Literature* (Chicago: University of Chicago Press, 1984), p. 13.

40. Gates, *Signifying Monkey*, pp. 64–65.

41. Baker, *Blues, Ideology, and Afro-American Literature*, p. 197.

42. Ibid., p. 195.

43. Adolph L. Reed Jr., *W. E. B. Du Bois and American Political Thought: Fabianism and the Color Line* (New York: Oxford University Press, 1997), p. 137.

44. Baker, *Blues, Ideology, and Afro-American Literature*, p. 177.

45. Ibid., p. 183.

46. Ibid., p. 190.

47. Ibid., pp. 190, 195.

48. Nor does one get very far if one makes the turn into cultural and diasporic studies generally. Paul Gilroy's characterization of a black diasporic politics merely repeats Park's description of the Negro as expressive. Gilroy writes that the

diasporic "movement can be identified by its antipathy to the institutions of formal politics and the fact that it is not principally oriented toward instrumental objectives. Rather than aim at the conquest of political power or apparatuses, its objective centers on the control of a field of autonomy or independence from the system." Paul Gilroy, "One Nation Under a Groove," in *Small Acts: Thoughts on the Politics of Black Cultures* (New York: Serpent's Tail, 1993), pp. 43–44. Maintaining the autonomy of black identity becomes an end in itself. Park is lurking not so far in the background here, either for Gilroy or for the whole of the cultural studies movement. See for example, Stuart Hall and Tony Jefferson, eds., *Resistance through Rituals: Youth Subcultures in Post-War Britain* (London: Hutchinson, 1976). Finally, Ellen Messer-Davidow remarks on the similarity between cultural studies and Chicago school sociology: "Whether labeled 'the Chicago School' or symbolic interactionism, . . . [i]ts emphasis on the complexities of the social construction of identity, on everyday life, on small groups—and their meaning-making and cultural innovation—as well as on culturally and linguistically sensitive field research, shows clear affinities to aspects of work in cultural studies. Indeed, early cultural studies work on subcultures at Birmingham references American work (mainly in the fields of delinquency and deviance) in this school." Ellen Messer-Davidow, "Whither Cultural Studies?" in *From Sociology to Cultural Studies*, ed. Long, p. 279.

Conclusion

1. Ralph Ellison, "As the Spirit Moves Mahalia," in *The Collected Essays of Ralph Ellison*, ed. John F. Callahan (New York: Modern Library, 1995), p. 252.

2. Ibid., pp. 254, 255.

3. Quoted in Jules Schwerin, *Got to Tell It: Mahalia Jackson, Queen of Gospel* (New York: Oxford University Press, 1992), p. 65.

4. Ellison, *Invisible Man* (1952; reprint, New York: Vintage, 1990), p. 453.

5. Ellison, "As the Spirit Moves Mahalia," p. 255.

6. Alan Nadel's "Ralph Ellison and the American Canon," *American Literary History* 13, no. 2 (summer 2001): 393–404, offers a largely positive reading of the novel.

7. Ralph Ellison, *Juneteenth: A Novel* (New York: Random House, 1999), pp. 98–99.

8. Ibid., p. 109.

9. Ellison, "As the Spirit Moves Mahalia," p. 255.

10. Robert Penn Warren, *Who Speaks for the Negro?* (New York: Random House, 1965), p. 345.

11. Ralph Ellison, "The Art of Fiction: An Interview," in *Collected Essays*, p. 217.

INDEX ....